"*Incarceration without Con*
understanding of mass i.   .... Rabinowitz compellingly
demonstrates, pretrial detention is both a key driver of imprisonment
and the cause of many of the same collateral consequences. This
book is essential reading for students and scholars concerned about
the impact of pretrial detention in the U.S. justice system."

*John Hagan, John D. MacArthur Professor of Sociology and
Law at Northwestern University*

"In *Incarceration without Conviction*, Mikaela Rabinowitz challenges
us to squarely face the issue of whether innocence does or doesn't
matter in the modern day criminal legal system. With pretrial detention leading so directly to convictions, and harsh incarceration
experiences visited upon her interviewees even if they're acquitted, Rabinowitz's questions about the value of America's vaunted
presumption of innocence are vital to confront."

*Vincent Schiraldi, Senior Research Scientist at the Columbia School
of Social Work and Co-Director of the Columbia Justice Lab*

Incarceration without Conviction

Incarceration without Conviction addresses an understudied fairness flaw in the criminal justice system. On any given day, approximately 500,000 Americans are in pretrial detention in the US, held in local jails not because they are considered a flight or public safety risk, but because they are poor and cannot afford bail or a bail bond. Over the course of a year, millions of Americans cycle through local jails, most there for anywhere from a few days to a few weeks. These individuals are disproportionately Black and poor.

This book draws on extensive legal data to highlight the ways in which pretrial detention drives guilty pleas and thus fuels mass incarceration—and the disproportionate impact on Black Americans. It shows the myriad harms that being detained wreaks on people's lives and well-being, regardless of whether or not those who are detained are ever convicted. Rabinowitz argues that pretrial detention undermines the presumption of innocence in the American criminal justice system and, in so doing, erodes the very meaning of innocence.

Mikaela Rabinowitz is the Director of Data, Research, and Analytics at the San Francisco District Attorney's Office, which does not seek to detain people using cash bail. She has a PhD in Sociology from Northwestern University and a BA in African American Studies from Columbia University.

Sociology Re-Wired

Edited by Jodi O'Brien, Seattle University, and
Marcus Hunter, University of California, Los Angeles

Sociology Re-Wired captures this combustible moment in American and global societies with new books that innovate and re-configure social and political issues. This hybrid series publishes timely, relevant, original research and textbooks that address significant social issues informed by critical race theory, Black feminism and Queer Studies traditions. Series books are written in a publicly accessible, multi-vocal style broadening the reach and impact of significant scholarly contributions beyond traditional academic audiences.

Some titles published in this series were published under an earlier series name and a different editorship.

Published:

The Black Circuit
Race, Performance, and Spectatorship in Black Popular Theatre
Rashida Z. Shaw McMahon

All Media Are Social
Sociological Perspectives on Mass Media
Andrew Lindner and Stephen R. Barnard

Incarceration without Conviction
Pretrial Detention and the Erosion of Innocence in American Criminal Justice
Mikaela Rabinowitz

Transforming Scholarship
Why Women's and Gender Studies Students Are Changing Themselves and the World
Michele Tracy Berger and Cheryl Radeloff

For more information about this series, please visit: https://www.routledge.com

Incarceration without Conviction

Pretrial Detention and the
Erosion of Innocence in American
Criminal Justice

Mikaela Rabinowitz

Routledge
Taylor & Francis Group

NEW YORK AND LONDON

First published 2022
by Routledge
605 Third Avenue, New York, NY 10158

and by Routledge
2 Park Square, Milton Park, Abingdon, Oxon, OX14 4RN

Routledge is an imprint of the Taylor & Francis Group, an informa business

© 2022 Taylor & Francis

Library of Congress Cataloging-in-Publication Data
Names: Rabinowitz, Mikaela, author.
Title: Incarceration without conviction : pretrial detention
and the erosion of innocence in American criminal justice /
Mikaela Rabinowitz.
Description: New York, NY : Routledge, 2021. |
Series: Sociology re-wired
Identifiers: LCCN 2020054374 | ISBN 9781032006185 (hardback) |
ISBN 9781032006192 (paperback) | ISBN 9781003174936 (ebook)
Subjects: LCSH: Arrest—United States. | Presumption
of innocence—United States. | Preventive
detention—United States.
Classification: LCC KF9625 .R33 2021 |
DDC 345.73/0527—dc23
LC record available at https://lccn.loc.gov/2020054374

ISBN: 978-1-032-00618-5 (hbk)
ISBN: 978-1-032-00619-2 (pbk)
ISBN: 978-1-003-17493-6 (ebk)

Typeset in Bembo
by codeMantra

For Lisa, Soraya, and Elliot

Contents

Series Editor's Foreword

Jails everywhere. Prisons everywhere. Any encounters with America's criminal justice system for Black and Brown communities are fraught at best, deadly and dangerous at the very least. Marshalling more than a decade of pioneering research, advocacy, and analyses, Dr Mikaela Rabinowitz's *Incarceration without Conviction* calls us to rewire and reframe our thinking about and understanding of crime, punishment, civil rights, and American justice in order to see how easily innocent people become entangled in the endless web of process whereby they await outcomes from America's local and county jails without bail. Where many scholars have emphasized the power and problems of America's prisons, *Incarceration without Conviction* demonstrates that for Black, Latinx, and poor and working-class people, America's jails are where their innocence and freedom are snatched away, stolen as their fate becomes the collateral damage of implicit and explicit biases among legal workgroups and criminal justice professionals. Long before bail and pretrial detention and their effects had entered into mainstream discussions of criminal justice reform, Dr Rabinowitz had logged years of detailed interviews and data analysis on the critical nature of bail in influencing justice outcomes for the most precarious and vulnerable. *Incarceration without Conviction* is the culmination of her path-breaking, necessary, and illuminating scholarship lighting the way to a freer, safer, and healthier criminal justice system and thus a better America.

Marcus Anthony Hunter
Sociology Re-Wired Series Editor

Acknowledgements

There are three people without whom this book would not have been written. Marcus Anthony Hunter spent the better part of the last decade insisting that my research and my voice deserved to see the light of day. He ignored my continued excuses that I didn't have time and didn't know how to write a book, never arguing with me, but also never letting the subject drop, demonstrating his faith in me and my work through his regular inquiries about my publication plans. When he became a series editor and began asking me for a prospectus, his combination of insistence and confidence helped me to overcome my self-doubt.

If Marcus gave me the confidence to embark on this process, Jean Beaman gave me the near constant moral and intellectual support to get it done. Whether by text, email, gchat, Twitter, or phone call, Jean was available to help me think through any challenge, somehow always knowing the perfect balance between giving advice and listening as I worked things out for myself. Jean is as close as anyone could be to a coauthor to this work.

And finally, but far from least, Lisa Magged, my partner, wife, and co-parent, with whom I have been navigating life since 2004. Lisa, too, had endless confidence in me and my work, and an absolute commitment to ensuring I got it done. Whether taking our kids away for a weekend so I could write in silence, copyediting chapters before I submitted them, or making me a cocktail when I needed a break, Lisa encouraged and supported me in more ways than I could possibly name.

Beyond these three are the many friends, colleagues, mentors, and mentees who have supported my professional and intellectual development, leading up to and through the writing of this book. I'd like to especially thank the two women who first introduced me to sociology and sociological thinking as an undergrad: Mignon Moore and Laurie Essig. Their mentorship and friendship were foundational as I developed the tools I needed to understand and describe the world around me. I was fortunate to have several incredible advisors in graduate school as well, foremost among them my dissertation committee chair, John Hagan, and committee members Art Lurigio, Monica Prasad, and Laura Beth Nielsen. Without their time, generosity, hard questions, and sage advice, I would never have completed my PhD. Mary Pattillo's guidance and support were also formative. The lessons I learned in her course on qualitative methods continue to inform my work, and Mary's continued interest in my progress and success during and after graduate school have always stood out to me.

In the decade-plus between graduate school and this book, I have learned an enormous amount about applied sociology, criminal justice policy, and the relationship between research and reform. Patricia Soung first introduced me to the youth justice movement and has continued to be an amazing friend and collaborator. Amid all of the work that remains to be done, I am glad to know that she and I will continue to be in it together. At RDA, Nishi Moonka and Amalia Freedman were the professional mentors I needed at the exact time I needed them, and Pat Bennett gave me opportunities I could not have gotten elsewhere. Friends and mentees Ardavan Davaran, Chris Ndubuizu, Thato Ramoabi, Debbie Mayer, Alison Hamburg, and Jasmine Laroche continually pushed me, helping me think through both methodological and normative assumptions. Working with all of them has made me a better researcher and advocate. In that vein, having the opportunity to work alongside David Muhammad, Vinny Schiraldi, and Jorja Leap was truly a blessing.

My time at Measures for Justice gave me critical exposure to the national landscape of reform-oriented research, as well as a brilliant cohort of colleagues, scholars, thinkers, and doers. Amy Bach's book provided particular inspiration, as have conversations and collaborations with Samantha Silver, Fiona Maazel, Gipsy Escobar, Sema Taheri, and the whole DO Team: Jennie Brooks, Lauren McQueen Pearce, Amanda Valtierra, and Shelby Davis.

My friend and unofficial colleague Lauren Willis gave me endless encouragement on our weekly hikes and helped me overcome my ambivalence about my qualifications for discussion issues of jurisprudence.

I need to acknowledge and thank my parents, Kay Edelman and Des Rabinowitz. Both were born and raised in colonial southern Africa—my mom in apartheid South Africa and my dad in Zimbabwe during a time when it was called Rhodesia. Both spoke frankly about race and racism, more than I think most White parents do, planting the seeds for my own interest in the ways in which our public institutions entrench racist hierarchies. My siblings, Vanessa and Darren, and stepparents, Dan Edelman and Kate Rabinowitz, have also been persistent sources of support and encouragement. Finally my children, Soraya and Elliot, whose boundless love, curiosity, silliness, and joy constantly inspire the same in me.

1   Introduction

On March 1, 2017, Spike TV began its six-part broadcast of *Time: The Kalief Browder Story*, a TV documentary detailing the experience of Kalief Browder, a young Black teenager who spent three years inside New York City's Riker's Island Correctional Facility because he was unable to afford $3000 in bail after being accused of stealing a backpack. From the age of 16 when he was arrested until the age of 19 when he was released, Browder maintained his innocence, refusing multiple plea bargains that would have expedited his release and freed him from the persistent physical and psychological violence and deprivation that characterized his life inside Riker's. Ultimately, the District Attorney's Office dropped the charges and Browder was released in May 2013. The years following his release from custody were plagued by post-traumatic stress and psychiatric breakdowns and, two years later, Kalief Browder took his own life, dying by suicide in June 2015.

As the Jay-Z produced documentary illustrates, Browder's experiences are exceptional and thus noteworthy—he was only 16 at the time of his arrest; the incident for which he was arrested was minor and the bail amount clearly disproportionate to the alleged offense; the detention facility in which he was held is one of the most notorious in the country; Browder's insistence on his innocence and unwillingness to take a plea deal were extremely rare; and the depth of Browder's trauma and his eventual taking of his own life are not the usual consequence of pretrial detention. In many more ways, however, Browder's experience was rote to the point of mundane. He was a young Black man arrested for a minor offense with the resources for neither private representation nor release on bail; Browder's bail hearing likely lasted no more than a couple of minutes, with neither the judge nor the prosecutor truly considering Browder's likelihood of appearance in court, risk to public safety, or ability to pay bail; the adjudication process was subject to numerous continuances and administrative delays that kept Browder in custody indefinitely; and ultimately, despite Browder never being convicted of the crime for which he was detained, the consequences of this detention were extreme.

Thus, however exceptional this case was, Browder's experience is also far too common. On any given day, approximately 500,000 individuals are in pretrial detention in the US, held in local jails not because they are considered a flight risk or a public safety risk, but because they are poor and cannot afford bail or a bail bond. Over the course of a year, millions of Americans cycle through local jails, most there for anywhere from a few days to a few weeks (Subramanian et al. 2015b). As with all aspects of the American criminal justice system, these individuals are disproportionately Black and poor (Nellis 2016; Subramanian et al. 2015b; Western and Pettit 2005).

Unfortunately, these individuals are also understudied, their experiences largely missing from the sizeable body of academic research on incarceration. Although the past decade has seen researchers within and outside of the academy paying more attention to pretrial detention, the depth and the breadth of this work still pales in comparison to scholarship on mass incarceration, punishment, or inequality. Moreover, research on pretrial detention has been limited by the almost total absence of qualitative research, which has meant that the voices and experiences of those who have been detained have not been a part of this work and have neither driven nor even really informed how scholars think about and understand pretrial detention.

Drawing on interviews with 67 individuals who were detained pretrial in Chicago's Cook County Detention Center and quantitative analysis of 5000 criminal court records from the Cook County Criminal Court, this book unmasks and explores a relatively hidden process endemic to mass incarceration: pretrial detention. In so doing, this book makes a series of arguments related to the social science and policy literatures on incarceration and to the function of the criminal legal system.

In terms of the former, this book argues that the study of pretrial detention is essential for understanding both mass incarceration and the collateral consequences thereof. Despite the wealth of scholarship on mass incarceration, this work has not sufficiently reckoned with pretrial detention either as a driver of prison growth or as a distinct form of incarceration that has grown alongside imprisonment. To date, most research on the emergence of mass incarceration has focused on prisons alone, with particular attention given to sentencing policy and other policies and practices that have put more people in prison and kept them there for longer (Alexander 2012; Mauer 1999; Schoenfeld 2018; Travis et al. 2014). The complementary body of collateral consequences research that has emerged to document the implications of incarceration for individuals, families, communities, and society has followed this trend, focusing both implicitly and explicitly on the collateral consequences of prison expansion and incarceration (Hagan and Dinovitzer 1999; Mauer and Chesney-Lind 2002; Middlemass 2017; Patillo et al. 2004; Western et al. 2004).

Incarceration without Conviction underscores how pretrial detention mirrors well-established patterns in mass incarceration and complicates common assumptions about those patterns. In particular, this book makes an important contribution to our understanding of the drivers of mass incarceration and their disproportionate impact on Black Americans, underscoring the ways in which front end criminal processes like pretrial detention drive back end processes like conviction and imprisonment.

Toward that end, *Incarceration without Conviction* addresses important questions raised by the growing body of research on pretrial detention, which has overwhelmingly found that being detained pretrial increases a defendants' likelihood of being convicted and, if convicted, of being sentenced to prison compared to similar defendants who are released pending adjudication (Lowenkamp et al. 2013; Oleson et al. 2014; Petersen 2019b; Petersen 2020; Schlesinger 2007). This book answers important questions raised by that research by shedding light on the mechanisms through which pretrial detention impacts case outcomes. Using a mixed methods approach that quantitatively measures the effect of pretrial detention on defendants' case outcomes and then draws on interviews with defendants who were detained about their case resolutions, this book reveals the reasons why pretrial detention is so strongly correlated with negative case outcomes. In addition, the diversity of circumstances of the individuals interviewed for this book—including whether they maintained their innocence or acknowledged guilt and whether they were cleared of wrongdoing or convicted of a crime—provides a unique opportunity to understand how people who are detained weigh a variety of considerations in deciding whether to plead guilty. Regardless of their actual guilt or innocence, individuals who are detained largely consider the same factors as they decide whether or not to plead guilty, including their jobs, their families, their conditions of confinement, their likelihood of prevailing in court, and the stigma of having a felony conviction.

Understanding how these decisions are made highlights the role of front end criminal justice processes—arrests, bail determinations, pretrial processes, etc.—in exacerbating the back end—i.e. mass incarceration.[1] Moreover, documenting the disparate rates of detention for Black versus non-Black defendants makes clear how these processes entrench and exacerbate the already dramatic overrepresentation of Black people in our criminal justice systems.

In addition, this book provides a needed adjustment to the research on the collateral consequences of incarceration, much of which inadvertently conflates the consequences of being incarcerated with those of having a felony conviction. Because *Incarceration without Conviction* explores the experiences of individuals who ultimately are convicted of the charges for which they were detained as well as individuals who are never convicted, this book is able to examine the ways in which being detained has financial, personal, and psychological consequences regardless of whether or not people are convicted of felonies or cleared of wrongdoing. In this way, this book also contributes to the growing body of research detailing the many ways in which even minor contact with the justice system can have far-reaching consequences, including Kohler-Hausmann's (2018) and Natapoff's (2018) respective work on misdemeanors, and work on legal financial obligations (LFOs) related to contact with the criminal legal system (Beckett et al. 2008; Martin et al. 2018; Shannon et al. 2020).

Finally, this book engages Supreme Court rulings and the associated law review literature on the nexus between the presumption of innocence, an "axiomatic and elementary" principle at "the foundation of the administration of our criminal law" (*Coffin v. US 1895*), and pretrial detention as a process in which legally innocent individuals experience circumstances otherwise reserved for people convicted of crimes. In particular, this book argues that the experiences and outcomes of individuals who are detained pretrial show the functional irrelevance of presumption of innocence, as defined by the Supreme Court and implemented in the American criminal justice system. Indeed, for individuals who are detained pretrial, neither actual nor legal innocence is a meaningful differentiator of process or outcome: during the pretrial phase, when all defendants are legally innocent, actual innocence has a minimal effect on whether or not an individual is convicted, as individuals who have not committed any crimes plead guilty following a series of encounters with the criminal legal system that lead them to believe that conviction is the only likely outcome. Moreover, for the small minority of people who are not convicted, both the fact of being detained and the collateral consequences thereof make their eventual acquittals or dismissals effectively meaningless. In addition, as this book shows, the consequences of being detained—both during and following detention—are largely identical regardless of legal or actual innocence, and include both material losses and psychological trauma.

Thus, the goal of this work is twofold: first, to add to the current body of academic research on incarceration and related issues like racial inequality, collateral consequences, pretrial detention, etc.; and second, to contribute to the larger body of work—academic and nonacademic research, journalism, popular media, etc.—drawing attention to the great injustice that is pretrial detention in this county in the hope that we can eliminate the systems and processes that have eroded the very meaning of innocence.

Below, I provide a brief overview of prior research on pretrial detention as well as a brief discussion of case law related to the presumption of innocence, bail, and pretrial detention.

A Brief History of Bail and Pretrial Detention in the United States

Bail is written into the American Constitution via the Eighth Amendment's prohibition on excessive bail, which implicitly acknowledges the desirability of pretrial release. Despite this, however, neither bail nor pretrial detention was the focus of much policy or research until the mid-to-late 1950s, when law professor and criminal justice reformer Caleb Foote began a series of studies on bail and pretrial detention, which soon found an interested audience in the form of a major policy-oriented philanthropist.

Directed by Foote and carried out by Foote and a cadre of his students from the University of Pennsylvania Law School, the 1953 Philadelphia bail study and the 1957 New York bail study set out to uncover the following issues related to setting bail and obtaining pretrial release:

> the effect of bail administration upon the accused with regard to the likelihood that he would be able to obtain pretrial conditional release, the standards and practices employed in setting the amount of bail, the impact of pretrial imprisonment upon the accused's ability to prepare a defense, the disposition of the cases of those subjected to pretrial imprisonment and the comparative dispositions of cases in which the convicted defendant had and had not been free on bail pending trial. (Foote 1959: 44–45)

Findings from both studies were very similar.[2] First, Foote found high rates of detention even for defendants charged with fairly minor crimes and low bail amounts. In addition, Foote and his students found that somewhere between 10 and 20 percent of defendants who were incarcerated pending adjudication were never convicted of the crimes for which they were held. In spite of not being convicted, these defendants spent anywhere from 13 to 149 days in custody. Finally, Foote found that defendants who were detained pending adjudication were significantly more likely to be convicted and, if convicted, significantly more likely to be sentenced to prison than defendants who were out on bail during the adjudication process.[3]

Although Foote acknowledged that these results were not necessarily causal given the numerous factors that affect case outcomes and sentencing, he argued that "the markedly similar differences [between the outcomes of detained and released defendants] obtained in both studies makes it difficult to escape the conclusion that pretrial incarceration disadvantages the accused in the disposition of his case" (1959: 47). He hypothesized a number of reasons for this disadvantage, including the likelihood that defendants who could not afford bail also could not afford private attorneys and so were dependent on overworked public defenders, the possibility that being incarcerated made defendants appear guilty in the eyes of various criminal justice administrators thus biasing their treatment, and the fact that detainees were limited in their ability to contribute to their defense because of constraints on their ability to meet with defense counsel and witnesses during detention.

Foote also highlighted a number of issues raised by his findings and by the practice of pretrial detention more generally. First, he pointed out that predicating defendants' pretrial freedom upon their ability to afford the cost of bail clearly amounted to economic discrimination. Although the explicit purpose of bail is to create a financial incentive to ensure defendants' appearance at court proceedings, in reality this objective can only be achieved if the defendant in question can afford this financial incentive; if not, bail functions as a mechanism of incarceration. Foote's two studies supported this, showing that cost of bail was based primarily on the severity of the crime(s) a defendant was charged with, so that poor defendants were regularly incarcerated based on charges for which more affluent defendants obtained release, in Foote's view violating constitutional guarantees of equal protection.

Second, he pointed out the conflict between the presumption of innocence as "a basic foundation of our criminal procedure" and the pretrial incarceration of defendants who have not been and may never be convicted (1959: 43). Regardless of a defendant's eventual disposition, "detention is demoralizing and oppressive" and pretrial detention constitutes punishment before conviction (1958b: 730). Moreover, Foote's interviews with detained defendants revealed that the punitive effects of pretrial detention were experienced not only by detainees themselves, but also by their families. This was particularly true when defendants lost their jobs as a consequence of their detentions and were unable to continue supporting their families (1954).

Finally, Foote noted as a practical concern that the conditions of pretrial detention were deplorable and noticeably more restrictive than the conditions imposed on convicted inmates in most prisons. Although this concern, unlike the aforementioned issues of economic discrimination and undermining the presumption of innocence, was not intrinsic to pretrial detention but rather the result of "administrative convenience" and inadequate funding for pretrial detention centers, it was no less disturbing, especially to detainees themselves (1959: 47).

By fortuitous coincidence, around this time, the issue came to the attention of wealthy industrialist and philanthropist, Louis Schweitzer. After hearing about a particularly egregious instance of a poor defendant being incarcerated for a prolonged period of time in lieu of nominal bail, Schweitzer began making personal inquiries into bail practices and pretrial detentions. His inquiries led him to Foote, among others, and resulted in his formation of the Vera Foundation (now the Vera Institute of Justice) for the primary purpose of financing research on bail and pretrial detentions.

In 1961, eight years after Foote's first bail study, the Vera Foundation commenced its first project, the *Manhattan Bail Project*, in collaboration with NYU School of Law and the Institute of Judicial Administration. Like Foote's studies, this project set forth to assess both the administration of bail and the effects thereof on defendants' pretrial custody status, case disposition, and sentencing. The results, cited in Rankin (1964), were unambiguous: "an accused who has been detained in jail between his arraignment and the final adjudication of his case is more likely to receive a criminal conviction or jail sentence than an accused who has been free on bail" (p. 641).[4]

Bail Reform, Part 1

The Vera Foundation's work on bail soon caught the attention of Sen. Sam J. Ervin, Jr, who chaired the Subcommittee on Constitutional Rights of the Senate Committee on the Judiciary, and Attorney

General Robert Kennedy. US Department of Justice (DOJ) research on bail processes and outcomes in a series federal districts had found that, depending on the district, anywhere from 23 to 83 percent of federal criminal defendants could not make bail and that across districts, "those detained prior to trial pleaded guilty more often than those free on bail, secured less frequent acquittals and dismissals, and were more likely to receive prison sentences than probation" (Freed and Wald 1964: 17). Following a series of small-scale investigations into issues affecting poor defendants in the federal criminal justice system, the DOJ formed a larger commission, resulting in the National Conference on Bail and Criminal Justice in May 1964. The DOJ and the Vera Foundation collaborated to prepare the conference and subsequent report, *Bail in the United States: 1964*, detailing the history and theory of bail and discussing the problems uncovered in the aforementioned research.

At the same time, Foote (1965a and b) published an extensive analysis of the constitutional concerns raised by pretrial detention, arguing that it was unconstitutional to detain defendants who could not afford bail. The congressional discourse on bail, as documented in Sen. Ervin's testimony from 1967, touched upon the same constitutional and empirical issues and evidenced overwhelming agreement with Foote's assessment.[5] After a couple of years of debate, all this attention culminated in the near-unanimous passage of the Bail Reform Act of 1966, which rewrote the Federal Rules of Criminal Procedure to "assure that defendants 'shall not needlessly be detained' prior to trial in federal criminal courts" by "create[ing] a presumption of release without payment of money before trial" (Wald and Freed 1966: 940). The primary innovation of the Act was to direct federal judges making bail decisions to include an evaluation of defendants' likelihood of absconding based on the strength of their community ties, as measured by their family ties, residential stability, and employment status[6] (Wald and Freed 1966).

A number of states soon followed suit, revising their bail decision-making criteria to include community ties and/or creating new bail options for judges to use, such as conditional release or deposit bail programs (Goldkamp 1985; Goldkamp and Gottfredson 1979). The former allowed for nonfinancial release under restrictive conditions similar to probation and parole, including limited supervision, curfews, and travel restrictions, while the latter, also called "10 percent bail," required the defendant to put down a deposit with the court of only 10 percent of his total bail in order to obtain release (Goldkamp et al. 1995).

Notwithstanding the revolutionary nature of these reforms, a number of scholars analyzing the implementation and impact of bail reform in the federal criminal courts and in various state court systems found problems, especially a high level of ambiguity and a lack of uniformity regarding the application of the new rules (Bock and Frazier 1977; Goldkamp and Gottfredson 1979). Moreover, despite reductions in the use of pretrial detention in some jurisdictions, in other jurisdictions, detention remained the norm.[7]

Bail Reform Backlash

Of course, all of this was happening amid the backdrop of a larger period of social and political change brought forth by the Civil Rights Movement.[8] As social unrest grew and the Civil Rights Movement gave way to the feminist movement, Black Power, anti-war protests, and more, a law and order backlash emerged, exemplified and intensified by Nixon's 1968 presidential campaign. Arguing that protests, riots, crime, etc. were the result of social disorder, Nixon and the Republican Party promised to restore "law and order," with Nixon himself claiming that "the 'solution to the crime problem is not the quadrupling of funds for any governmental war on poverty but more convictions'" (quoted in Beckett 1997).

In spite of the near-universal support for federal bail reform in 1966 and the subsequent enactment of similar reforms across the country, the law and order backlash that swept the country soon came for bail reform. Despite little evidence associating released pretrial defendants with crime, the push to revise bail policies and place greater emphasis on "public safety" grew, fostered by growing attention on street crime and law and order politics, and encouraged by extensive media attention on crimes committed by individuals out on bail.[9] In addition, while the bail reform movement of the late 1950s and early 1960s had looked at bail only as a means for ensuring defendants' appearance in court, the backlash movement argued that bail should also be used to keep criminals off the streets (Goldkamp 1979, 1985). Politicians, prosecutors, and law enforcement criticized the new rules as overly permissive towards criminal defendants and insufficiently protective of the safety of the general populace.[10]

When Congress passed the District of Columbia Court Reform and Criminal Procedure Act of 1970, the tide had officially begun to turn. As Sen. Ervin noted with disappointment, the DC crime bill "mark[ed] the symbolic, if not the actual end of an extraordinary decade of criminal law reform," by turning the focus of criminal

justice policy away from civil liberties and towards crime control
(1971: 291). The DC crime bill was the first ever "comprehensive
preventive detention law in the United States," and explicitly allowed judges to deny bail to defendants whom they considered likely
to commit crimes while out on bail as well as to consider dangerousness and likely criminal activity in the determination of financial
bail (Goldkamp 1985: 5). Sen. Ervin lamented that the DC bill was
"an illustration of what happens when politics, public fear, and cre-
ative hysteria join together to find a simple solution to a complex
problem" (1971: 292).

The battle between supporters of release-oriented bail policies and
supporters of more restrictive bail policies persisted throughout the
1970s, with many states initially liberalizing their bail laws to encourage pretrial release, only to add more restrictive provisions that
encouraged greater use of detention and/or more restrictive release
conditions a few years later. By the early 1980s, restrictive bail policies had clearly won, and 34 states and the District of Columbia
had passed provisions that allowed judges greater leeway to deny
bail to defendants they deemed dangerous and instructing judges to
prioritize defendants' dangerousness and communities' safety in the
determination of bail amounts and release conditions (Goldkamp
1985). At the national level, congress responded by replacing the Bail
Reform Act of 1966 with the Bail Reform Act of 1984, which, like
many of the state reforms that preceded it, was most noteworthy for
its explicit allowance for the preventive detention of defendants not
charged with capital crimes.

In the face of criticism by civil libertarians and other advocates,
supporters of preventive detention argued that by allowing judges
to deny bail to the most high-risk defendants, the new bail reforms
would eliminate the widely used but unofficial judicial practice of
using high bail fees as a means of *sub rosa* preventive detention and
thus actually reduce the number of low-risk defendants detained
pretrial (Goldkamp 1985; Jones 1989; Wanger 1987).

This argument, however, quickly proved to be incorrect. Research conducted by the General Accounting Office on federal
pretrial detention three years after the 1984 Bail Reform Act
found that the total percentage of defendants detained had actually risen slightly, from 26 percent to 31 percent, and that in some
districts more than three-quarters of all people detained pretrial
were in custody because they could not afford their financial bail,
not because they had been determined too dangerous to release
(Jones 1989).

Pretrial Detention Today

The 20 years following the 1984 Bail Reform Act saw the greatest increase in incarceration in American history and is the period of time most commonly associated with the rise of mass incarceration. While the dramatic growth of the American prison population has garnered the most attention, jail populations also grew enormously, driven primarily by the detention of unconvicted pretrial defendants (although the number of convicted individuals in jail serving short sentences also increased during this time). As the Vera Institute report *Incarceration's Front Door: The Misuse of Jails in America* found, between 1983 and 2013, jail admissions almost doubled, increasing from 6 million to 11.7 million (Subramanian et al. 2015a).[11] Over roughly the same period of time, the proportion of people in jail who were unconvicted increased from 50 to 62 percent (Perkins et al. 1995). Cumulatively, the increase in pretrial detention populations has been extreme. In 1983 a BJS jail census found that 113,984 unconvicted individuals were incarcerated in local jails awaiting adjudication (Perkins et al. 1995). By 2008, this number had more than quadrupled to 494,300 (Minton and Sabol 2009).

Amid this increase, the past 15 years have seen a growing body of research on pretrial detention, focusing primarily on the effect of pretrial detention on criminal justice outcomes. While specific findings have varied based on the study sample, jurisdiction, etc., the research has been overwhelmingly conclusive in demonstrating the negative effects of pretrial detention on case outcomes, including both convictions and sentence severity (Heaton et al. 2017; Oleson et al. 2014; Petersen 2020; Sacks and Ackerman 2012; Williams 2003). In addition, research has indicated that racial disparities in pretrial detention explain some of the racial disparities in conviction and sentencing outcomes (Hart 2006; MacDonald and Raphael 2017; Martinez et al. 2020; Omori and Petersen 2020; Petersen 2020; Petersen and Omori 2020; Schlesinger 2007). In other words, Black defendants are more likely to be detained pretrial than other defendants, which then increases the likelihood that they will be convicted and receive a more severe sentence.

Using data collected from the Bureau of Justice Statistics (BJS), the Prison Policy Initiative found that pretrial detention also disproportionally affects women, especially Black women. "In stark contrast to the total incarcerated population, where the state prison systems hold twice as many people as are held in jails, *more incarcerated women are held in jails than in state prisons*" (Kajstura 2019, emphasis original). More than 60 percent of these women are in jail pretrial, and more than 80 percent of them are mothers, the majority of whom are also their children's primary caregivers.

Notably, much of the research on pretrial detention over the past two decades has come not out of academia, but out of criminal justice agencies and policy research organizations. For example, the New York City Criminal Justice Agency (NYCJA) recreated Foote's early New York Bail Study, this time with a much larger dataset and with more advanced statistics (Phillips 2007, 2008, 2012). Looking at more than 40,000 cases that proceeded through New York City's Criminal Courts between Oct. 1, 2003 and Jan. 31, 2004, their analysis found that pretrial detention status had large and statistically significant effects on all rates of conviction, carceral sentences, and sentence length for both felony and misdemeanor defendants. Based on these findings, NYCJA made several recommendations to reform bail practices, including increasing non-monetary release in the form of both release-on-recognizance (ROR) and supervised release, in addition to recommendations for statutory changes to the New York State's bail laws to better differentiate between defendants who should not be released because they pose too high a risk to public safety from those who would be released if they could afford bail.

Other researchers have also used findings around the negative impact of pretrial detention to advocate for reform. Amid these efforts, there have been signs of progress over the past decade, with both states and counties undertaking changes to their bail and pretrial release practices. For example, a 2013 report on New Jersey jail populations by the Drug Policy Alliance spurred statewide reforms to bail and pretrial practices; in 2017, New Jersey overhauled its bail and pretrial processes, creating a statewide pretrial services agency, introducing procedural protections regarding preventive detention, and mandating the use of pretrial risk assessments to inform release and detention decisions. In the past five years, Alaska, California, Illinois, New Mexico, Maryland, and New York have all passed various versions of bail reform, although rollbacks in several states make clear that this battle is far from over. Nonetheless, many local jurisdictions, which lack the jurisdiction to make major statutory overhauls, have experimented with various pretrial service programs to reduce the number of unconvicted people behind bars solely due to their inability to pay, and both left- and right-leaning policy and advocacy organizations are drawing attention to the inherent inequity of basing someone's detention status on his or her ability to pay.

If recent attention to this issue by media and private philanthropy is any indication, other states are likely to follow suit. In the last year or two, local and national news media as varied as the New York Times, the Durham North Carolina's Herald Sun, and the Cleveland Jewish News (to name a few) have all published recent articles criticizing the unjustness of money bail, many driven by local efforts to overhaul bail processes. Major national foundations, such as the MacArthur Foundation and the Charles Koch Institution, are investing in local and national bail reform initiatives, and businesses are paying attention too: in 2018, both Facebook and Google announced that they would no longer publish ads from bail bond organizations, citing the harm this industry brings to low income communities of color.

In short, the time is ripe for academics to pay greater attention to these issues as well. Caleb Foote's work on this topic, almost 70 years ago now, was critical for the passage of the 1966 Bail Reform Act. More recently, academic research on mass incarceration and the extensive collateral consequences thereof has been an important part of a shifting public narrative on public safety and incarceration, one which recognizes that putting more people in prison for longer periods of time does not actually promote public safety, but rather destroys lives and communities.

Pretrial Detention vs the Presumption of Innocence

Does the very act of detention conflict with the presumption of innocence? What happened to Kalief Browder lends support for arguments on both sides: on the one hand, Browder was ultimately cleared, the charges against him dropped, indicating that the presumption of innocence remained, even amid his long detention. And yet nothing in Browder's experience remotely resembled any casual understanding of how an innocent person would be treated.

The question of whether the pretrial detention of individuals who have not been convicted of a crime conflicts with the presumption of innocence as a foundational principle in American law has long been asked by lawyers, scholars, and policymakers working on issues related to bail and pretrial detention. Of course, as I show throughout this book, to the actual people who are detained, this question is, at best, absurd: in practice it is obvious to any detained person that he/

she is always presumed guilty and that this technical presumption is made meaningless by the material reality of detention. Nonetheless, it is valuable to understand what the law says on the topic.

The presumption of innocence was enshrined in American law in 1895 via a Supreme Court holding in *Coffin v. United States*, in which the Court ruled that a lower court judge had erred by refusing to instruct a jury that the defendants in the case were innocent until proven guilty. After detailing the lengthy history of the presumption of innocence from the Old Testament through Greek, Roman, and British law, the Court declared that the "presumption of innocence in favor of the accused is the undoubted law, axiomatic and elementary, and its enforcement lies at the foundation of the administration of our criminal law." This clear statement notwithstanding, operationalizing this concept was complex and, again detailing historical jurisprudence, the Court defined the presumption of innocence as "evidence in favor of the accused" and tied it to "the doctrine of reasonable doubt," noting that evidence in favor of conviction must be stronger than the presumption of innocence to be beyond a reasonable doubt. Nothing in this decision addressed the issue of pretrial detention, but three subsequent cases did explicitly address the intersection between the presumption of innocence and the pretrial incarceration of legally innocent people: *Stack v. Boyle* (1951), *Bell v. Wolfish* (1979), and *US v. Salerno* (1987).

In *Stack v. Boyle*, a group of defendants who had been charged with conspiring to violate the Smith Act[12] contested the bail set by the District Court. After several different motions to reduce bail were dismissed, they filed a request for review by the US Supreme Court. The petitioners argued that their bail, which was set at $50,000 per person, violated the Eighth Amendment's prohibition against excessive bail given their financial resources and low flight risk. The Court agreed and explicitly tied this to the presumption of innocence, noting, "Unless this right to bail before trial is preserved, the presumption of innocence, secured only after centuries of struggle, would lose its meaning."

This ruling notwithstanding, bail determinations beyond defendants' ability to pay remained a common occurrence. In 1979 the Supreme Court fundamentally redefined the presumption of innocence and laid the foundation for the current reality in its ruling in a class action suit brought by individuals detained pretrial in New York City's Metropolitan Correctional Center (MCC). In *Bell v. Wolfish*, individuals who were detained pretrial at MCC challenged the legality of conditions they experienced in detention, claiming that double-bunking, restrictions on reading materials, cavity searches, and shakedowns amounted to punishment before conviction. Both District and Appellate courts largely agreed with plaintiffs, but the Supreme Court did not. Instead, the Court noted that notwithstanding the punitive experience of detained individuals, their detentions served a regulatory function, not a punitive one, and thus did not legally constitute "punishment." In addition to determining that uncomfortable conditions of pretrial detention did not constitute punishment before conviction, the Court also addressed and un-ambiguously rejected the contention that pretrial detention violated the presumption of innocence, ruling that "The presumption of innocence is a doctrine that allocates the burden of proof in criminal trials," and, as such, "it has no application to a determination of the rights of a pretrial detainee during confinement before his trial has even begun."

In 1987, the Supreme Court further entrenched the legitimacy of pretrial detention in *US v. Salerno*, upholding the 1984 Bail Reform Act's provisions allowing the government to detain an individual before trial. The law in question was one that allowed for the intentional "preventive" detention of allegedly dangerous individuals through the denial of bail, rather than somewhat more incidental pretrial detention of individuals who cannot afford bail, but the Court's ruling still had repercussions for the latter, and more common, form of pretrial detention. In addition to ruling that the Eighth Amendment prohibition against excessive bail does not constitute a right to bail, the Court also cited the *Bell v. Wolfish* decision in noting that if the intent behind pretrial detention is not punitive, the detention cannot be determined to be punishment.

In a forceful dissent, Justice Thurgood Marshall called out the majority's ruling as "sophistry" and took issue with the illogic of almost every argument therein (*US v. Salerno* 1987). He took particular umbrage with two arguments in the majority ruling: first, the notion that the regulatory intent of pretrial detention precluded any consideration of its punitive effect and, second, what he viewed as effective elimination of the presumption of innocence. Summing up his scathing critique of the "absurdity" of the majority, Marshall concluded:

> Throughout the world today there are men, women, and children interned indefinitely, awaiting trials which may never

come or which may be a mockery of the word, because their governments believe them to be "dangerous." Our Constitution, whose construction began two centuries ago, can shelter us forever from the evils of such unchecked power. Over 200 years it has slowly, through our efforts, grown more durable, more expansive, and more just. But it cannot protect us if we lack the courage, and the self-restraint, to protect ourselves. Today a majority of the Court applies itself to an ominous exercise in demolition. Theirs is truly a decision which will go forth without authority, and come back without respect.

I dissent.

This book is also intended as a dissent to the absurdity and sophistry intrinsic in the idea that pretrial detention does not constitute punishment or make meaningless the presumption of innocence. I will come back to both of these ideas again throughout the subsequent chapters. First, I provide a brief discussion of my research methodology before providing an overview of the rest of the book.

Getting to the Facts

This book is based primarily on interviews with 67 individuals who had previously been detained pretrial in the Cook County Department of Corrections, aka the Cook County Jail in Chicago, IL. Where relevant, interview data is supplemented by quantitative data from the Cook County Clerk of the Circuit Court. Both are discussed in further detail below.

I recruited study respondents at various Cook County Courthouses; through social service agencies, including inpatient and outpatient drug and alcohol treatment programs; on internet message boards; and by word of mouth.[13] Per Institutional Review Board (IRB) Human Subjects guidelines, respondents had to be at least 18 years old to participate.[14] All respondents had to have spent at least two nights in jail following an arrest but without having been convicted of that crime; the majority had been detained much longer, with most respondents having been detained for at least a month and about one-quarter having been detained pretrial for six months or more. Most respondents had been detained once in their lives, although approximately one-third had multiple detention experiences. In the case of respondents who had experienced multiple pretrial detentions, each detention was addressed separately in the interview. The charges for which respondents had been arrested ranged from shoplifting to murder, although by far the majority were either drug possession or domestic violence. I interviewed 39 Black men, 7 White men, 14 Black women, and 7 White women, who ranged in age from 18 to 60.

While the demographic distribution of this sample broadly mirrors the demographics of the jail population, it is not perfectly representative and should be understood as a convenience sample rather than a random sample. The absence of Latinx individuals in the qualitative sample is a particular shortcoming, since the quantitative sample (below) indicates that around 14 percent of defendants are Latinx. That said, the extreme overrepresentation of Black respondents relative to the overall county population is an almost exact mirror of the disproportionately Black county jail and criminal defendant populations. According to the 2010 census, 24.8 percent of the County population is Black, compared to 55.4 percent White and 24.8 percent Latinx (of any race). The overrepresentation of Black people in the jail and criminal defendant populations is so big that all other racial/ethnic groups are underrepresented relative to their proportion of the population.[15] This disparity has a number of implications, which I discuss throughout the book.

Interviews addressed a wide range of topics, including respondents' arrest, detention, and court experiences; employment status and economic wellbeing before and after detention; interactions with attorneys; relationship and contact with family and friends during detention; case outcomes and sentence; and more. The interviews were conducted in semi-private locations, such as a neighborhood library branch, a community center, or an office at the courthouse, and lasted from 30 to 90 minutes; all but two were recorded.

The statistics that supplement the interview data are based on data from the Cook County Clerk of the Circuit Court. Five thousand cases were randomly selected from the Cook County criminal courts records for 2005. Of these, 4,322 had complete data for analysis and, of these, 2,624 proceeded to prosecution in felony criminal courts. (The remainder had their charges dropped or reduced to misdemeanors, in which case the charges were pursued in a separate division of the circuit courts.) Detailed information is provided for each of the 2,624 cases, including defendants' demographic characteristics, alleged offenses, legal representation, pretrial custody status, case outcomes, sentence type (carceral, fine, probation), and more. Descriptive characteristics of the sample are shown in Table 1.1.

Table 1.1 Descriptive characteristics of felony defendants in Cook County
criminal court

Categorical Characteristics	N	%		
Race				
Black	2093	79.8		
Latino	364	13.9		
White	167	6.4		
Gender				
Male	2242	85.4		
Female	382	14.6		
Legal Counsel				
Public Defender	1728	65.9		
Private Attorney	896	34.1		
Detention Status				
Detained Pretrial	1221	46.6		
Released Pretrial	1403	53.5		
Continuous Characteristics	*Mean*	*Range*	*SD*	
Age	31	16–66		10.47
Number of weeks from arrest until final court date	32.78	0–216.86		29.46

Overview of Chapters

The following four chapters are conceptually organized into two
sections: Chapters 2 and 3, which separately consider individuals
whose cases result in criminal convictions (Chapter 2) and those
whose do not (Chapter 3); and Chapters 4 and 5, which discuss these
two groups in concert. This organizational structure is designed to
1) highlight distinct practical and analytic considerations regarding
detained individuals who are ultimately determined to be legally
guilty compared to those who are not, and 2) underscore the com-
monalities between these two groups.

Chapter 2, "The Mechanics Of The Guilty Plea," focuses on the
primary issue examined in scholarship on pretrial detention: the fact
that individuals who are detained are more likely to plead guilty
than those who are released. In contrast to the majority of research,
which focuses almost exclusively on documenting this fact, this book
seeks to understand *why* pretrial detention is so strongly correlated
with criminal conviction—a topic about which much has been
hypothesized but little has been studied. In so doing, *Incarceration*

without Conviction highlights the mechanisms through which front end criminal legal processes, like arrest and detention, drive back end processes, like conviction and incarceration, as well as how these front end drivers exacerbate the disparities in outcomes between Black and White defendants. This chapter uses a random sample of criminal court record data from the Cook County Circuit Court to corroborate prior scholarship and show that individuals who are detained pretrial are more likely to be convicted, and then draws on qualitative data on respondents' decisions to plead guilty to explain why this is, using interviews with individuals who pled guilty while detained to shed light on their decision-making process. By drawing on the experiences of individuals who chose to plead guilty despite insisting on their innocence as well as individuals who plead guilty while acknowledging some amount of engagement in illegal activity, this chapter shows how the experience of engaging with the criminal legal process erodes people's belief that that they have any chance of prevailing in court, and how this experience is exacerbated by their confinement.

In addition, this chapter draws attention to the role of pretrial detention in exacerbating negative outcomes for Black defendants relative to defendants from other racial/ethnic groups. Using a series of regressions, this chapter shows how the disproportionate detention of Black defendants, in combination with the negative effect of detention on case outcomes, drives higher rates of conviction for Black defendants.

In Chapter 3, "But What Will Become Of The Innocent?" I turn from those individuals who ultimately plead guilty to what is perhaps the most understudied—and yet ethically egregious—aspect of pretrial detention: the pretrial detention of people who are ultimately not determined to have committed a crime. Here, more than in any other chapter, I take on the legal discourses on punishment and innocence, highlighting the inadequacy of the legal definitions of both in relation to the lived realities thereof. Detailing the experiences of five of the individuals I interviewed who were never convicted of any crime, including a 17-year-old boy who was found not guilty at trial after nine months of detention and several other respondents whose charges were dropped anywhere from a few days to a few months after they were first detained, this chapter highlights the paradox between the legal presumption of innocence and the lived experience of punishment. In addition to documenting the punitive experience of detention for these innocent individuals, this chapter also shows the other consequences of pretrial detention on people's lives, livelihood, and wellbeing, and foreshadows the issues of both material loss and psychological harm that are discussed more extensively in Chapters 4 and 5.

Having used the experiences of those who plead guilty to show how pretrial detention drives incarceration and racial inequities in Chapter 2 and the experiences of those never convicted to illustrate how it belies the lived reality of constitutional protections in Chapter 3, I turn to examine the shared experiences of these two groups in Chapters 4 and 5. Using the literature on the collateral consequences of incarceration as a starting point, these chapters highlight the harm caused by confinement regardless of legal outcome.

Chapter 4, "Someone Has to Pay a Price...," focuses on the material harm that pretrial detention inflicts, showing how being detained erodes people's financial security and economic wellbeing in ways that have consequence during and after the actual detention. Regardless of whether or not they were convicted, the individuals I interviewed lost their jobs when they could not show up for work and lost their homes when they missed rent payments. For poor people, who comprise the majority of those detained, even quantitatively small costs have qualitatively large consequences, which affect family members at home as much as those held in jail. This chapter builds on and expands scholarship on collateral consequences by showing how many of the material consequences of incarceration—often associated with having a felony conviction—are equally real for people who are not convicted of crimes.

Finally, in Chapter 5, "The Pains Of Imprisonment," I emphasize the psychological and personal toll—the trauma—of pretrial detention on detained people and their families. Like Chapter 4, this chapter adds important nuance to existing scholarship on the collateral consequences of incarceration by showing how even relatively brief detentions, including those that do not result in a felony conviction, are emotionally and psychologically damaging to the individuals who are detained and to their families. In addition to the trauma of being detained and associated depression, anger, and anxiety, this chapter also shows the toll of pretrial detention on people's faith in the criminal justice system. Drawing on the scholarship on procedural justice, this chapter explores the ways in which the injustices that detained people face undermine the legitimacy of the justice system more generally.

The sixth and last chapter of this book summarizes the findings detailed in the prior four chapters and provides a synthesis of their theoretical and practical implications. Toward this end, this chapter revisits the relationship between pretrial detention and mass incarceration, showing how the former contributes to the latter. I also revisit the collateral consequences of detention and the issues of innocence and punishment, highlighting the hollowness of the former given the extensiveness of the latter. This chapter concludes with a discussion of the policy implications of this book, with particular attention to current efforts to change bail practices and reduce pretrial detention populations. Current practices in this country, by and large, are a disgrace, but they do not have to stay that way.

Notes

1 In this way, this book is also a complement to the growing body of work on prosecution, which also draws attention to the effect of front end processes—in that case, filing of criminal charges and other discretionary prosecutorial decisions—on back end outcomes such as incarceration (Bazelon 2019; Pfaff 2014, 2017, 2020).

2 For the Philadelphia study, Foote and his students used different samples from various stages in the criminal process to analyze the outcomes of defendants charged with both misdemeanor and felony offenses, while the New York study involved a single, but much larger, sample of only felony defendants. Statistical analyses in both studies were supplemented with interviews with defendants who were unable to obtain bail as well as with bail bondsmen and various criminal justice officials. In spite of the different locations, populations, and sampling techniques in these studies, their results were remarkably consistent: first, Foote and his students found that a significant proportion of defendants were unable to afford their bail and, consequently, were held in jail pending the adjudication of their cases. Fifty-eight percent of felony defendants in the New York study were incarcerated pretrial, while in Philadelphia, where less accurate sampling required estimation, approximately 75 percent of defendants accused of serious crimes were detained. Moreover, Foote found high rates of detention even for defendants charged with fairly minor crimes and low bail amounts; in New York, 28 percent of defendants whose bail was set at $500—the standard amount set for minor charges—were detained because of their inability to pay, while in Philadelphia, where misdemeanor defendants were included in the study, the percentage of defendants detained pretrial was 15 percent and 32 percent in state and federal courts, respectively (Foote 1954, 1958b, 1959).

3 In the Philadelphia sample of more serious offenses, 48 percent of detained defendants were convicted compared with only 18 percent of released defendants (Foote 1954, 1959). Of convicted defendants in Philadelphia, 59 percent who had been detained were sentenced to imprisonment compared with only 22 percent of those who were out on bail; in New York, these numbers were 84 percent and 45 percent respectively.

4 In addition, Rankin conducted a more rigorous multivariate analysis to better isolate the effects of pretrial detention and demonstrate a causal

relationship between being detained pretrial and negative criminal justice outcomes. Controlling for prior criminal record, bail amount, type of counsel, family ties, and employment status, she found that pretrial detention had strong, statistically significant positive effects on the likelihood of both conviction and receipt of a carceral sentence.

5   Foote argued that pretrial detention based on high bail was unconstitutional on four grounds: people who were detained were denied 1) the fundamental fairness guaranteed by the due process of the law because they are being punished by imprisonment prior to being tried; 2) procedural due process because pretrial detention negatively impacts case outcomes, depriving defendants of their right to a fair trial; 3) equal protection of the law because of the denial of pretrial liberty only on the basis of economic status; and 4) the right to bail under the Eighth and Fourteenth Amendments, violated because the proscription against excessive bail means that bail should not be set so high as to eliminate defendants' fundamental right to freedom pending adjudication.

6   The Bail Reform Act also allowed for consideration of the nature and circumstances of the charges, prior convictions, prior record of court appearance, and preponderance of evidence against the defendant, but it was the focus on community ties, with an emphasis on releasing defendants with strong ties regardless of their financial resources, that differentiated the Act from previous bail laws (Miller 1970).

7   Bock and Frazier (1977) found that despite recommendations that judicial officers consider the length and character of defendants' residence in the community; their family ties; their reputation, character, and mental condition; the willingness of other community members to vouch for their reliability; and more, bail determinations were still made almost exclusively based on the severity of the charges and the defendant's prior criminal record. Goldkamp and Gottfredson (1979) analyzed the effect of variables including demographic characteristics, employment status, prior record, community ties, and more on the outcomes of defendants' bail hearings and found that the majority of variance could not be explained by any of these factors. They concluded that the new rules requiring the consideration of numerous factors were so lacking in specificity regarding their actual application that they essentially reinforced judicial discretion rather than facilitating rationality and uniformity.

Thomas's (1976) evaluation of the effectiveness of bail reform ten years after the passage of the Federal Bail Reform Act showed mixed results. In an extensive study of pretrial detention in 20 US cities that had reformed their bail guidelines to emphasize pretrial release, he found that the total percentage of felony defendants detained throughout the entirety of their adjudication had decreased by one third over the previous decade, while the total percentage of misdemeanor defendants detained had decreased by almost 25 percent. In addition, he noted that although failure to appear rates had increased, they had increased at a much lower rate than the detention rates, indicating that the majority of released defendants were not flight risks.

Nonetheless, the rates of pretrial release varied widely across jurisdictions and had actually increased in several jurisdictions, indicating that the application of the new rules was far from consistent and that, for many defendants, bail continued to be unaffordable. The 1970 National Jail Census confirmed this, showing that more than half of the people in US jails were still unconvicted defendants awaiting adjudication.

A National Institute of Justice (NIJ) evaluation of pretrial release in eight geographically and demographically diverse state court jurisdictions found that even amid increased rates of release almost 90 percent of released defendants appeared at every required court hearing. Less encouragingly, the study also found that almost 17 percent of released defendants were rearrested during the pretrial period (Toborg 1981).

8 Sen. Ervin was a segregationist Southern Democrat, whose commitment to civil liberties for individuals involved in the federal criminal justice system did not extend to a commitment to civil rights for African Americans in Southern states.

9 Research on crime committed by defendants out on bail produced widely divergent results, with one congressional study showing 7.5 percent of felony defendants being rearrested while another showed a 70 percent rearrest rate for robbery defendants. Most research fell close to the 10 percent range (Thomas 1976).

10 Writing only three years after the passage of federal bail reform, the Assistant US Attorney for the District of Columbia argued that by releasing too many defendants, the new rules were fueling high rates of recidivism among defendants out on bail, and that many of the conditions that judges were now encouraged to attach to defendants' release, such as curfews and travel restrictions, were largely unenforceable (Miller 1970). Although the 1966 Bail Reform Act and similar pro-release state statutes did not apply to capital defendants and did allow judges to deny bail to individuals accused of capital crimes, critics argued that these limitations did not go far enough and pushed for new guidelines that allowed judges greater latitude to deny bail and emphasized issues such as dangerousness, public safety, and likelihood of recidivism as the most important bail criteria (Goldkamp 1985; Miller 1970; Wanger 1987). No attention was paid to the majority of released defendants who neither recidivated nor absconded (Goldkamp 1985).

11 This increase was not driven only by changing pretrial detention practices, but also by the array of other policy practices changes identified in the extensive research on mass incarceration.

12 The Smith Act criminalized advocating the overthrow of the US government by force or violence and required all non-citizen adult residents to register with the federal government. Defendants in *Stack v. Boyle*, who were members of the Communist Party, were accused of the former.

13 Word-of-mouth recruitment was especially effective with Black respondents, almost all of whom had friends and/or family members who had had similar experiences.

14 Illinois is one of the few states that allows 17-year-olds to be held in adult jails.

15 Van Cleeve (2016) details the pervasive anti-Black racism in Cook County's criminal justice system in all of its unique specificity and disturbing generalizability.

2 "The Mechanics Of The Guilty Plea"[1]

Almost all criminal cases end with a guilty plea. In 2011, the Department of Justice's Research Summary on Plea and Charge noted that between 90 and 95 percent of federal and state court cases are resolved through a guilty plea (Devers 2011). While there is no data on the proportion of these pleas that come from individuals who are detained, the evidence that being detained pretrial increases the likelihood of pleading guilty is overwhelming and incontrovertible. To date, the vast majority of research on pretrial detention has focused on the relationship between pretrial detention status and case outcome. *Every study that has been done on the topic* has found that individuals who are detained pretrial are more likely to be convicted than individuals who are released pending adjudication— even when controlling for relevant case and defendant characteristics (Hart 2006; Heaton et al. 2017; MacDonald and Raphael 2017; Martinez, Petersen, and Omori 2020; Oleson et al. 2014; Omori and Petersen 2020; Petersen and Omori 2020; Sacks and Ackerman 2012; Schlesinger 2007; Williams 2003). Independent of all other factors, pretrial detention drives higher rates of conviction and incarceration.

The Cook County Criminal Court system is no different. Criminal Court records from 2005 show that among individuals arraigned on felony charges, those charges were either dismissed or reduced to misdemeanors for 49 percent of defendants who were out on pretrial release, compared with only three percent of defendants who were detained pretrial. Moreover, among those defendants whose charges were not dismissed or dropped to misdemeanors, 91 percent of defendants who were detained pretrial were convicted, compared with only 82 percent of defendants who were released during the adjudication process.

Controlling for both legal and non-legal factors that are generally associated with criminal convictions and other negative criminal justice outcomes offers an even more disturbing picture: defendants who are detained throughout the adjudication process have 218.8 percent greater odds of being convicted than defendants who are not detained. Moreover, pretrial detention status is by far the most important factor in determining whether or not a defendant will be convicted, outweighing the also large and highly significant effects of characteristics such as offense type and having a public defender, and completely eliminating any disparate outcomes tied to race (see Table 2.1).[2]

The question, of course, is *why?* Why is being detained pretrial more strongly associated with being convicted than any other defendant or case characteristic? To answer this question, I turn to the experiences of Reggie,[3] Helen, and Gavin, three of the individuals I interviewed who pled guilty, despite insisting on their innocence. This discussion is layered with the experiences of Brandon, Mark, Sarah, and Thomas, all of whom did report some form of criminal behavior but plead guilty to more serious charges than appropriate considering their actual actions, or in pleading guilty accepted more serious criminal penalties than would be expected for the kind of offense they committed.

As these interviews show, immediately following their arrests and arraignments, almost all defendants intend to fight their charges and prove their innocence or, in cases where defendants acknowledge some wrongdoing, demonstrate mitigating circumstances such as substance use disorders and seek treatment or other supportive

Table 2.1 Defendants who are detained pretrial have higher odds of being convicted

Variable	Odds Ratio	SE
Black	1.289	0.139
Age	1.043	0.034
Age squared	0.999	0
Public Defender	1.779★★	0.203
Drug Charges	1.219★★	0.063
Weapons Charges	1.105	0.04
Property Charges	1.937★★★	0.169
Violent Charges	1.026	0.036
Detained	2.188★★★	0.125
Constant	2.226	0.564
★ p < .05	★★★ p <.001	

services. As they move through the criminal process, however, defendants' interactions with the criminal justice system make clear the irrelevance of their guilt or innocence to system actors who focus more on efficacy than on uncovering the facts of a case. For individuals who are detained, this experience is made worse by the circumstances of their detentions, including reduced access to defense counsel and the fact that by being in jail they are essentially living the consequence of being guilty. Ultimately, their experiences with the court system and related actors erodes people's belief that they have any chance of being acquitted while leading to the realization that since they are already being treated like they are guilty, they may as well plead that way.

Reggie

On Dec. 12, 2008, Reggie was walking from a friend's apartment to the bus when he asked some guys standing on the corner if they could break a $100 bill for him. Two police officers observed the exchange and approached Reggie and the men with whom he had made the exchange. Reggie admits he knew that the people he exchanged money with were on the corner dealing drugs, but points out that there is nothing illegal about exchanging money.

> I was in a hurry to get to the bus. I had like $230 in my pocket and I was trying to get some change. I knew they was out there hustling, doing they thing, so I asked them could they change a $100 bill for me. He said yeah, no problem. So, he gave me the change and in the process of him giving me the change some of it ended up being marked money. So, as we decided to part company and go our separate ways the police converged on us and when they come up, they searched me, they threw me on the car, they didn't just search me. Threw me on the car, patted me down and told me they seen me making the exchange of money. I told them "yeah you did, no problem about that. I ain't got to hide that. But the thing of it is, he was changing money for me. It wasn't like I was buying nothing." Then from that process on they said, "well let me check the money." So they checked the money and when they checked it they called it "marked money"… He told me because of the fact that I had that marked money, it meant I was out there selling drugs and at the time, like I say, I wasn't doing nothing. I was minding

my own business but I did need the change for the bus. I tried to explain it to the officer. He didn't care to hear that. So they went on and they arrested me.

Reggie was taken down to the local police station and charged with Delivery of a Controlled Substance before being transferred to the county courthouse for bond court the following morning. At the courthouse, he was placed in another holding cell with about 150 other men who had been arrested in the last day or two. A representative from the public defender's office came by and spent about an hour gathering basic information from everyone – what was everyone's name, age, and employment status, did they have children or other dependents, were they military veterans. Each person had about 30 seconds to tell the public defender's representative anything the public defender might be able to present to the judge to encourage leniency in bail determinations.

When Reggie's name was called, a county correctional officer told him to keep quiet and escorted him out of the holding cell and in front of the judge. The prosecutor told the judge that Reggie had previously been convicted of misdemeanor drug possession, and the public defender pointed out that he was an army veteran, a father of one, and a long-time resident of the area. The judge set his bail at $50,000 "D," and the correctional officer pulled him back into the holding cell. The whole process had lasted less than a minute.

The fact that Reggie was given a "D-bond" meant that instead of putting up the whole amount, he only needed to make a bail deposit of 10 percent in order to be released. Usually this would not have been a problem, but he had recently been laid off and, although he was receiving unemployment, finances were tight and he did not have an extra $5,000 for bail. After everyone had appeared in front of the bail judge, he was taken to Cook County Jail along with all the other defendants who did not have money for bail.

After several hours of intake processing at the jail, he was put in a cell in the medium security division and allowed to use one of the pay phones to make a phone call, his first one since he had been arrested 36 hours before. He managed to get through to his mother and asked her to get in touch with his 20-year-old son, whose phone did not accept collect calls. Although Reggie was upset about being locked up, he was not initially concerned about the criminal charges, assuming that they would be dismissed in three weeks when he went before the judge for his preliminary hearing. When he was taken to court for his preliminary hearing, however, Reggie discovered that he was being charged along with the guys he had been arrested with.

Knowing that the co-defendants were guilty, Reggie did not want to be tried along with them and requested that the judge separate his charges from theirs. The judge granted his request but gave Reggie a three-week continuance so the court could assign him a public defender who was not also representing the other defendants. Three weeks later—six weeks after Reggie was arrested—he went before the judge again for his preliminary hearing and, to his dismay, the judge found probable cause to pursue the charges. After the hearing, his public defender told him that his chances did not look good but that if he agreed to plead guilty, she could probably get him a good deal, advice that he immediately turned down.

> She was like "well, if you just go out here and admit that you're guilty, I could get you off with this." I was like: "you got to be crazy, you got to be crazy! I'm not going to admit to something I'm not guilty of."

At this point Reggie was getting worried. He could not collect unemployment while he was detained and he was concerned about money. He was also worried about his mother and his son; his mother had been living alone since his father passed away a few months ago and she was not in great health. Although his son had never been in any kind of trouble, Reggie worried that he was setting a bad example.

> [My son] is 20 now. One of the things I was worried about with him, even though he's a good kid, kids of the generation now they're easily influenced without a father figure around in they life. They can always pick up on the peer pressure and be hanging out in the streets. I didn't want to see that happen to my son, without me being around. I was pretty much worried about that. I didn't want him to get lost out here. Then my mom, her health wasn't all too good. I didn't want to be locked up and just by chance she pass away and I'm stuck, what can I do. There were a lot of things I was worried about that I knew I had no control over… They shut [my unemployment] down because I wasn't able to report in. I lost out on the rest of the unemployment by being locked up.

He was also frustrated with the court process and unhappy with his public defender. He kept demanding trial but every time he showed up for a court appearance, the judge gave him another continuance. He had no contact with his public defender between court appearances and when he saw her in court, she focused on plea bargain options, indicating to Reggie that she either did not believe or did not care about his innocence.

As the process dragged on, Reggie became increasingly despondent. He was stressed out about money, he was worried about his son and his mother, and he was lonely. Despite his loneliness, Reggie also felt more ambivalent about getting visitors as he was in jail longer, pointing out that it got harder and harder to see family members come and go when he could not. "It's hard to get a visit when you see your family and your relatives come see you in there they got to leave and you can't leave."

As Reggie and I sat talking, and he recounted the stress and loneliness of his time in jail, he suddenly paused, as if taking a step back and reflecting for a moment. When he resumed, Reggie started on a different topic, mentioning for the first time that he had been in the Army when he was younger, that he had been stationed in Lebanon for a while, "living in ditches for weeks at a time." After that experience, he told me, he thought he had the physical and mental resilience to be OK in any situation. After a couple of months in jail, however, he realized he was wrong: nothing could have prepared him for the stress and degradation of being detained.

> Being in the military and being in jail, you can't really compare the two together like that, because living in a ditch is not the same as somebody degrades your manhood from being in jail. That's a completely different situation there. It's not a good feeling at all.

When Reggie was given the opportunity to participate in the jail's drug treatment program, he decided it was worth getting out of the house of corrections side of the jail and into the drug treatment center where conditions were better, even though he worried that participating would look like he was conceding guilt. He also figured that it would look good in front of the judge since he did have a prior drug conviction, even though he continued to maintain his innocence regarding his current charge. The judge was duly impressed and after he had been in the drug program for several months, the judge offered him a deal that he could not refuse:

> She said 'you know what, I really believe you're working on something and what I'm willing to do, if you're willing to make a deal, you admit to being guilty that you had the money, I'll release you today, give you probation, and put you in the vet program [a special probation program for veterans].'
> Author: You took that?
> Yeah.

I asked Reggie why he finally agreed to plead guilty after five months of insisting on his innocence and how he felt about the outcome of his case.

> It was easier for me to take that than for me not to take it. Because if not, I would still be sitting there waiting or I'd be downstate in one of the state penitentiaries and I wasn't ready to go downstate to one of the penitentiaries. I got a young son. Well, he's not that young anymore, but I still got a family to take care of.
> Author: What was that like for you, or how did that feel? Copping to something?
> I didn't feel good about it at all because it's like I'm sitting there lying to myself. But, if I don't tell this lie to myself then… It's like I'm damned if I do and damned if I don't. I'm stuck either way I go regardless as to what I say or what type of proof I can come up with, it don't make a difference to the justice system. The justice system says you're guilty, you're guilty.

Reggie's experience largely exemplifies the experiences of other respondents who decide to plead guilty despite maintaining their innocence. When the process began, he assumed it was a relatively simple error and felt confident that the various system actors would recognize his innocence. Even as the process began to stretch out longer than he expected and it became clear that this was not the case, Reggie was aghast at the idea of pleading guilty to something he did not do. As time wore on, however, a combination of factors began to erode his commitment to proving his innocence, including loneliness, financial anxiety, and increasing despondence tied to the inherently degrading experience of being incarcerated. Moreover, concurrent to these depressing experiences, another realization surfaced: "…regardless as to what I say or what type of proof I can come up with, it don't make a difference to the justice system. The justice system says you're guilty, you're guilty."

The Courtroom Workgroup

Research indicates that Reggie was right: the criminal justice system generally functions to promote guilty pleas. As noted at the beginning of this chapter, the vast majority of cases that proceed through to disposition (versus being dismissed by prosecutors or judges prior to disposition) are resolved through a plea bargain, in which a defendant agrees to plead guilty in exchange for the prosecutor seeking less than the maximum possible sentence. In federal courts, a full 97 percent of criminal cases end in a plea bargain and, while data are harder to come by for state courts, recent research shows this number to be well over 90 percent (Gramlich 2017; Gramlich 2019; Jones et al. 2018). There are a number of reason that explain this trend, including the coercive power of prosecutors, who have significant discretion in how they charge defendants and can threaten more serious charges for defendants who do not plead guilty, and the trial penalty, which shows that individuals who go to trial and are convicted receive more punitive sentences than individuals who plead guilty to the same charges (Pfaff 2017; Jones et al. 2018; Bazelon 2019).

Another critical explanation and one that is of particular relevance here is the "courtroom workgroup," the collaborative relationship between prosecutors, defense attorneys, and judges who work together to maximize efficiency and collegiality (Eisenstein and Jacob 1977). Despite of the ostensibly adversarial nature of the American justice system, observers—including criminal defendants—have long noted that, in reality, these courtroom actors work together to promote the best shared outcomes for the court process rather than in an adversarial manner to produce the best outcomes for their respective clients.[4] This working relationship takes for granted the assumption that most defendants are factually guilty, and thus plea bargains are the best outcome for all involved.[5] As the people I interviewed made clear, the defining characteristic of their interactions with the court process and courtroom actors was the persistent push toward a guilty plea and plea bargain that would accompany it. This realization eroded any initial assumptions that they were presumed innocent, that they could prevail in court, or that there was any real way out besides pleading guilty.

Almost everyone I interviewed expressed adamant opposition to the idea of pleading guilty when first arrested and even when initially booked into the jail. For those individuals who were innocent of any form of criminal behavior, the most common initial response was one of shock and disbelief, coupled with the certainty that what

was happening to them was a mistake that would be quickly recti-
fied. At these initial points in the process, most people do not even
consider the possibility of pleading guilty, assuming that someone—
the prosecution, the police, the judge, *someone*—will recognize the
obvious error of what has happened and will correct it.

Of course, not all defendants are factually innocent. Many of the
individuals I interviewed did acknowledge engaging in some sort of
criminal behavior, sometimes the exact thing that they were being
charged with and sometimes an action that was less serious than
the criminal charges alleged. Regardless, they began the criminal
process with the belief that the judge would be a neutral arbiter of
a fair process in which they were defended by a defense attorney
committed to proving their innocence or, at the least, helping them
navigate the process and fighting for their best interests. People's experiences with the court and courtroom actors, however, undermine
these idealistic notions as people begin to realize that the courtroom
process is focused more on expedience than on a thorough determination of innocence or guilt.

"[The Judge] Like, 'This Girl Guilty.'"

For some defendants, this realization comes through their interactions with the judges assigned to their cases. Helen, a Black women
in her 30s, was pulled over for a minor traffic infraction while
driving her boyfriend's car, only to find out that the car was stolen.
Arrested for possession of a stolen motor vehicle, she was certain that
she could easily clear things up as soon as she appeared in court. "All
I needed was 2–3 minutes to tell [the judge] I didn't know my boyfriend stole my car, I didn't know the car was tagged. It wasn't my
fault." Having never been involved in the justice system but having
watched her fair share of TV courtroom dramas, Helen believed that
the judge, as the arbiter of guilt or innocence, would see past the
inaccurate criminal charges and recognize her innocence. After a
couple of court appearances, however, Helen quickly discovered that
the court process gave her little opportunity to profess her innocence
and, more importantly, no one seemed to care. "[The judge] didn't
want to listen to you at all. When I would want to open my mouth I
couldn't, I had to stop. He didn't want to even listen to me. I always
thought that was unfair. I know they have a lot of cases to listen to
but some people really are telling the truth. Some people, not many,
are honest. Some people are really innocent…"

As her interactions with the court accumulated, Helen's experience began to belie her early belief that her innocence was obvious;

instead, she began to realize that to all of the courtroom actors, she was guilty. "It's supposed to be justice. You're supposed to be able to go in there and speak... I felt like [the judge] just knew I was guilty. He like, 'this girl guilty.' Yeah." Convinced that she was not getting a fair hearing, Helen pleaded guilty, a decision she regrets several years later even though she thinks it was her only option.

For Gavin, a Black man in his late 20s, his very first interaction with the court—his bail hearing—was enough to make it clear that he was presumed guilty. Like Helen, he noted that the judge had little interest in hearing from him or other defendants and generally seemed more interested in moving the process along quickly than in a thorough understanding of what happened.

> It's an early morning court call, you know, 4–5 o'clock in the morning. So this judge really don't want to be up, so they ain't really trying to hear what's really going on because you, they figure you guilty but who wants to stay in jail.
>
> Author: And they treat you like you're guilty?
>
> Oh yeah, oh yeah.
>
> Author: Like how so? What makes it clear that they think you're guilty?
>
> When they set your bond up to $50,000, $70,000, $80,000. Who got that type of money! So they know they put your bond that high, I don't have no $70,000.

From a legal process perspective, of course, a bail hearing is not the appropriate venue in which to hear evidence and adjudicate the veracity of the charges, and legally a bail determination has no bearing on a determination of guilt or innocence. Case law has spoken directly to this question of the relationship between pretrial detention and the presumption of innocence and the Supreme Court has declared "the presumption of innocence 'allocates the burden of proof in criminal trials... but it has no application to a determination of the rights of a pretrial detainee during confinement before his trial'" (*United States v. Salerno*). To Gavin, however, the fact that the judge set his bond at an amount clearly beyond his means was an obvious indication that the judge presumed his guilt.

Others with direct experience with pretrial detention have long shared Gavin's sentiments. Jeff Thaler (1978), an attorney with the criminal appeals bureau of the Legal Aid Society, wrote that for his clients the ubiquity of pretrial detentions made into a "myth" the notion that a defendant is presumed innocent until proven guilty. In reality, he argued, "a person's presumed innocence is overcome by an arrest or indictment" as well as by "a bail proceeding where a magistrate uses the severity of the unproven offense to predict whether, if released, the accused will flee or commit a crime" (p. 441).

Three weeks after bond court, Gavin came back to court for his arraignment hearing and pleaded guilty.

> So I just copped out what they said.
>   Author: You just copped out as soon as you could so that you could get out?
>   To get out of there that day.

"PD Stands for Penitentiary Delivery"

Interactions with judges are not the only experiences that convince defendants that innocence matters less than efficiency and an admission of guilt is the most efficient outcome. More than their interactions with anyone else, defendants' interactions with their public defenders convince them that, as far as the process goes, they are presumed guilty.

Like Reggie's case described above, for many individuals I spoke with, their primary recollections of their public defenders centers on the role of their attorneys in the plea bargain process. Brandon's experience, described below, sums up the perspective of many of the respondents I interviewed. A Black man in his mid-30s, Brandon's encounters with the criminal justice system stemmed from an untreated substance use disorder. At the time of our interview, Brandon had been sober for several years and, with the benefit of therapy and introspection, understood his substance use disorder as a coping mechanism during a difficult transition to adulthood. Despite Illinois's commitment to treatment services and non-punitive approaches for people with substance use disorders who end up in the criminal justice system, however, Brandon noted that over the course of several years and multiple run-ins with the criminal justice system, no public defender ever tried to understand his circumstances enough to advocate for any support. Instead, as indicated by the courtroom workgroup literature, public defenders worked to encourage guilty pleas and expedite the court process.

> I'm sure you've heard this: we call the PDs "penitentiary delivery." They get you to cop out… Most of us who have prior experience with the criminal justice system still haven't learned how it works, but like that saying goes, ignorance is no excuse before the law. But we don't know our rights, so we can't defend ourselves.[6]

> My PD, she came in, she hung my record over my head, she said, "you're already on probation, you should just take the 3–5 [years being offered by the prosecutor]." I probably could have fought it because I had an addiction, but I didn't know that. I had no knowledge of how to fight, how to pull in resources for myself, and the PD offered nothing but time in the pen[itentiary].

Mark's description of his interactions with his public defender echo Brandon's. Like Brandon, Mark acknowledged some guilt, but expressed frustration that his attorney was more focused on convincing him to plead guilty than on understanding what had happened and why, and using the information to help Mark.

"[The public defender] did not represent me the right way, he did not," Mark told me. When I asked him to explain why he felt that way, Mark immediately pointed to his attorney's emphasis on plea bargaining, identifying this as the primary reason why he decided to plead guilty:

> I pleaded because up there with them [saying], "you going to trial you gonna lose, you gonna lose."
> Author: Your lawyer told you that?
> Yeah, basically. In so many words. They don't tell you outright like "you gonna lose," in so many words. They break it down to like "we can get you a lesser charge, we can get you the lesser time, but on the same charge we can get you lesser time. We gonna plea bargain for this."

Given his frustration with his lawyers' emphasis on plea bargaining, Mark decided to inquire about having a new attorney assigned to his case. The judge's response largely confirmed Mark's growing suspicion that all of the court actors were working together, and none of them was working for him.

> I asked to change my venue—change my venue of my lawyer. But the judge, how the court system is, the judge make you seem like, well, if you do that it's gonna take, you gonna sit in the county jail longer than what you have to because it's a long process. You got to fill out paperwork and then you got to see what public attorney, public defender is going to take, take your case—well we call, we don't call them public defenders, we call them "public pretenders." Because you pretending to protect me. You pretending to fight for my rights.

In addition to their shared disillusionment with their public defenders (and associated use of catchy disparaging nicknames), Brandon and Mark's quotes also evidence another pattern common among Black men who I interviewed: in discussing their experiences with the criminal justice system, Brandon and Mark—and a number of other Black male respondents—regularly moved back and forth between "I" and "we," the first person singular and the first person plural. Brandon's statement, *"we* don't know our rights, so we can't defend ourselves," and Mark's, *"we* call them 'public pretenders'"(emphasis added), underscore a reality about pretrial detention that reflects the reality of mass incarceration and all forms of criminal justice system contact—these are experiences are not randomly distributed, nor are they uncommon for certain segments of the American population. Rather, being detained in custody without having been convicted of a crime is a relatively common occurrence among Black men, especially Black men in low income Black neighborhoods, despite being uncommon among the larger American population. As Table 1.1 in Chapter 1 shows, the vast majority of individuals prosecuted for felonies in Cook County are Black. This disproportionality is even greater when looking at defendants who are detained: Criminal Court records indicate that 30 percent of Black defendants were detained pretrial, compared with 24 percent of Latinx defendants and 19 percent of White defendants. Looked at another way, out of 1221 detained felony defendants in a random sample of Cook County Criminal Court records, 1018—or 83 percent—were Black. Meanwhile, as noted in Chapter 1, according to the 2010 census, 24.8 percent of the County population is Black, compared to 55.4 percent White and 24.8 percent Latinx (of any race). As I discuss later in this chapter, understanding the dramatic overrepresentation of Black men—as well as Black women—in the pretrial detention population is critical for understanding how racial disparities are entrenched—and, as Omori and Petersen (2020) argue, institutionalized—through a process that is race neutral on its face and deeply racialized in reality.

Prejudice of Pretrial Detention

While interviews with individuals who were detained pretrial make clear the ways in which their encounters with the courtroom workgroup influence their decisions to plead guilty, it is also likely that, in some ways, the experiences described above are not unique to individuals who are detained. As noted above, the vast majority of criminal cases end in a guilty plea and it is likely that defendants who are out of custody are similarly disillusioned by the criminal court process with its emphasis on efficiency and associated promotion of plea bargains. These experiences, however, are exacerbated by being detained, which further limits defendants' contact with counsel, leads to encounters with additional criminal justice practitioners who presume their guilt, especially correctional officers, and subjects them to the very consequence they would experience if convicted.

In the case of detained defendants, this presumption of guilt is further exacerbated by what Caleb Foote (1954, 1958b, 1959) termed "the prejudice of pretrial detention," or the ways in which being detained pretrial undermines the fairness of the criminal process. Foote identified three ways in which pretrial detention prejudices case outcome: 1) factors of special prejudice, namely that the fact of being in custody makes defendants who are detained appear more guilty to various criminal justice system actors; 2) prejudice created by unnecessary conditions of pretrial detention, or ways in which detention conditions that are standard but not inevitable, such as poor physical conditions of pretrial detention facilities, incentivize defendants to plead guilty regardless of the facts of their cases; and 3) inevitable prejudice in any form of detention, or inherent concomitants of pretrial detention that negatively affect case outcomes, such as the fact that detained defendants cannot hold jobs, but holding a steady job is one of the primary ways a defendant demonstrates his reliability to the court and consequently inclines judges, juries, and prosecutors toward leniency.

More than 60 years later, this typology remains the primary framework for conceptualizing the mechanisms by which pretrial detentions harm defendants' case outcomes.[7] At the same time, given the exponential growth of the criminal justice system, increased rate of plea bargains, and growth of pretrial detentions, Foote's typology also underestimates the ways in which being detained pretrial exacerbates the systemic presumption of guilt that all defendants experience. In other words, while Foote is correct that being detained is a fundamentally different and obviously worse experience than going through the court process while out on bail, because he was writing at a time when the criminal justice process was less punitive and less centered around compelling guilty pleas, he also does not pay as much attention to the ways in which pretrial detention exacerbates aspects of the criminal process that are already working to produce guilty pleas. In particular, being detained involves communications barriers that make it difficult for defendants to contact their defense counsel, which furthers the already strong perception that their attorneys do not have their best interests at heart. In addition, staff inside the jail make it clear that they believe individuals are detained because they are guilty, thus exposing these defendants to another criminal justice system actor who also presumes their guilt. Beyond these two exacerbating experiences, being detained despite not being convicted demonstrates to defendants that the system views them as guilty by subjecting them to the very consequence they would incur if convicted, ultimately undermining any meaningful difference in a finding of guilt or innocence and thus reducing the value of insisting on one's innocence while increasing the benefit of pleading guilty.

"I Don't Think Anybody in There Get Contacted by a Lawyer"

For people who are detained pretrial, barriers to communicating with public defenders while in custody reinforce the disillusionment prompted by their attorneys' emphasis on pleading guilty. Sixty years ago, Foote (1954, 1958b, 1959) observed that limitations on contact with counsel while in custody precluded detained defendants from working with their attorneys to adequately prepare their defenses. Today the prevalence of plea bargains and the reality of public defender caseloads belie that idealistic notion that public defenders and their clients regularly communicate in a collaborative effort to mount a vigorous defense. Nonetheless, for defendants who are detained, the difficulty of contacting defense counsel adds insult to the already injurious process and furthers the realization that pleading guilty is the only viable option.

For Mark, whose dissatisfaction with his public defender is discussed above, the inability to get in contact with the public defenders' office likely served to prolong his time in custody, causing him to abandon his initial commitment to fighting his charges in the interest of expediting his release. For reasons that were never made clear to Mark, he waited more than three months following his initial arraignment before having another court hearing. While in jail, he had no access to information on the case processing, nor any way to contact an attorney who could help.

> I'm sitting there not knowing what's going on. I don't know nothing about no court date. I haven't got no court papers from anybody. So I'm sitting there for like three and a half months already.

Author: Did anyone, so did you have any kind of interaction with anybody from the courts during that time? I mean were you ever contacted by a lawyer or anything like that?

That's the, that's the one thing, I don't know. I didn't get in contact. I don't think anybody in there get contacted by a lawyer. But, sitting in there, it's like, it's the worst feeling. And they not letting you know anything of what's going on. No lawyer, the only time he comes speak with you is when you're in court, when you're back in the holding cell, in the bullpen[8] waiting to see the judge. That's when they come to you like, "okay, this what the District Attorney is offering. Either you take it or you leave it."

While the extended delay between hearings that Mark experienced was unique in its extremity, it is nonetheless worth noting that not a single individual who I interviewed recalled being visited by his or her attorney while in custody and those who tried to reach out to their attorneys were unable to do so due to the expense of making phone calls from jails.[9] Beyond underscoring the perception that people's assigned attorneys are not committed to helping their clients mount the most vigorous possible defense, the fact that defendants do not communicate with their attorneys while in custody means that their communications are restricted to brief interactions that occur only at court hearings. These crowded, brief, and harried interactions allow for no exchanges beyond discussions of current plea bargain options, again reinforcing defendants' views that their attorneys are encouraging them to plead guilty.

Thomas expressed similar frustration, noting that he asked everyone he interacted with how he could get in touch with an attorney but that there did not seem to be any way for him to do so. An African American man in his 50s, Thomas's experience echoed Brandon's in many ways. He acknowledged that he had forged a check, but explained that he had done so to support his heroin addiction. He hoped that he would be able to talk to his public defender about his substance use disorder and find treatment options but, like other defendants, found that conversations centered on plea bargain options.

[The public defender] asked me about my background, asked me what I want to do, am I pleading guilty or what they had to offer me and stuff like that. He didn't actually, he didn't tell me

that they had evidence, he didn't say nothing like that. He just
told me, "what you want to do? You want to plead guilty?" like,
"let's go and get the case over with. Plead guilty." Like that. He
didn't talk to me, he didn't say "let's fight the case." Nothing
like that. He really didn't seem to me like he was too enthused
about it. You know, like he had no interest in mine at all.

Despite wanting to talk to his attorney about treatment options,
Thomas kept finding that their interactions at the courthouse were
too rushed to have any meaningful conversations or discuss anything
specific to Thomas or his case.

He never spent any time with me so he really didn't know
nothing about me or how did I feel about the case or anything.
The only time was right before we go in [to the courtroom], he
come [talk to me] and the way he did it is that he—in the bullpen, he have at least 10–15 people he talk to and we talk right
there. He pull you out and talk right there, say "we got this and
this and that." And "what you want me to do?"

When I asked Thomas if he had tried to reach out to his attorney
between court dates, he made clear the futility of these efforts. "He
don't come to see you [in jail]." I pushed him to elaborate:

Author: And there was no way for you to contact [the public
defender's office]?
No, because they don't give you no phone [and] you can't
make a collect call to them… it's 3 weeks to 4 weeks before your
next court appearance. And you really don't, even if you get in
touch with your family they don't know, they don't have, they
don't give you nobody to call. They don't give you no information to the public defender's office or anything like that. So, you
basically sitting there, wondering what's going to happen. So
you learn to sit there and just don't say nothing. You get upset,
you can't do nothing, there's nothing you can do.

After six months in jail, 3–4 court hearings, and 3–4 harried conversations with his attorney, Thomas plead guilty, accepting a three-
year prison sentence with credit for time served, plus three years of
probation. Between the 6 months credit and time off of his sentence
for good behavior, he was out of prison in 61 days—having been in
custody three-times longer pretrial than post-conviction. Within a

year he was rearrested for drug possession, showing not only the absurdity of the pretrial detention but also the futility of the whole process.

"It's Your Fault You in Here"

Of course, the critical differentiating factor between defendants who are detained pretrial and those who are released is the basic fact of being in custody. More than anything, the very fact of being detained makes clear to people that the justice system and the actors therein presume their guilt by subjecting them to the very circumstance that is otherwise reserved for those who are convicted. Throughout the course of these detentions, correctional officers regularly make it clear that they view people's presence in jail as an indicator of their guilt, reinforcing the somewhat less explicit messaging detained individuals receive through their interactions with other system actors and belying the pretense that an acquittal is a realistic possibility. Numerous respondents recalled the punitive way they were treated while in custody and the effect of that treatment.

Mark tied comments by correctional officers presuming his guilt to his treatment in the courts to explain why he felt like he never had a chance of beating his charges despite his professed innocence:

> The first thing the officers say, "you wouldn't be, if you was innocent you wouldn't be in here." That's the first thing they say. "If you was innocent you wouldn't be in here." And you treated like basically you guilty. Until, you guilty until proven innocent. Until the court says, the judge says, by, if it's not enough credible evidence or witness, credible witness, that's when you free to go. If there's not enough incriminating evidence against you. But, other than that you just sitting in there.

Sarah, a middle-aged Black woman who was arrested for drug possession, also recalled correctional officers telling people directly that they would not be in jail if they were not guilty. Beyond these comments, however, Sarah spoke of how the whole experience conveyed to her and to others how they were viewed.

> When you use the washroom, it's like the washroom is right here and you got women sitting right there, I mean, if you want to have a bowel movement or anything or if you on your menstrual or anything, you don't want anyone looking at you. You

know, that's private. So in a way, it's like you just feeling real violated because of how they treat you and then—don't get me wrong. I have, when I was locked up in the jail, ran into some nice officers. All sheriffs is not mean and nasty but a lot of them are. You know, they cuss at you, they call you out your name, treat you like you some kids. And they always say, like "it's your fault you in here." And then when you try to explain the situation, like, "well I came out my house and I was walking down the street to the store and by my area is a high drug area,"… And it's wrong. It's real wrong.

Gavin was even more explicit about the connection between the punitive experience of being in custody and the decision to plead guilty, even referring to his detention as being "give[n]… time," as if it was a sentence following a conviction.

It make it worser because you locked up. It's a lot of people that really did done things but when you really have a person that really didn't do anything, it makes it worser. You want to, I might as well have went on and did it, y'all gonna give me all this time anyway when I really didn't do it. So that's why you get us behind these bars, the guards treat you like crap, so the first thing you thinking about going to court, cop out and get, get out of this place.

Ultimately, for most individuals who are detained, accumulation of interactions with criminal justice practitioners who convey their assumptions of defendants' guilt—or at least their disinterest in any outcome beyond a guilty plea—aligns with the reality that, by being detained, defendants are already experiencing the consequence of being convicted. To paraphrase Reggie earlier in this chapter, realizing that the justice system says they are guilty, defendants decide to plead guilty.

Pretrial Detention: Building On and Exacerbating Racial Inequality

As noted earlier in this chapter, the people I interviewed regularly referenced the fact that the vast majority of the people held in Cook County Jail were Black. Notwithstanding the pervasive overrepresentation of Black people across all domains of the criminal justice system in Cook County and elsewhere, pretrial detention is unique in that it is both a cause and effect of racial inequalities in the criminal justice system. As noted in the previous chapter, a number of studies have observed that Black defendants are more likely to be detained pretrial than White defendants and, because individuals who are detained are more likely to be convicted and receive more punitive sentences, racial disparities in pretrial detention explain some of the racial disparity in conviction and sentencing outcomes (Hart 2006; MacDonald and Raphael 2017; Martinez et al. 2020; Omori and Petersen 2020; Petersen and Omori 2020; Schlesinger 2007).

Cook County is no different. Black defendants are detained pretrial more often than Latinx defendants or White defendants and, as a consequence, are overrepresented within the pretrial detention population, above and beyond their representation in the overall felony court system (see Tables 2.2 and 2.3).

These numbers, however, actually obscure the true nature of the disparate effect of pretrial detention on Black Americans. Conducting a multivariate analysis that measures the relationship between racial group membership and pretrial detention status shows that, when controlling for other relevant characteristics, racism has an even greater effect on whether a defendant is detained. Using a logistic regression, which measures odds of being detained pretrial given a variety of defendant and case characteristics, shows that Black defendants have odds of being detained pretrial that are almost two-thirds greater (58 percent, to be exact) than White or Latinx defendants,

Table 2.2 A higher percentage of Black defendants are detained than other defendants

Race	Percent detained (N)	Percent Released (N)
Black	48.6 (1018)	51.4 (1075)
Latino	37.6 (137)	62.4 (227)
White	39.5 (66)	60.5 (101)

Table 2.3 Black defendants disproportionately comprise the pretrial detention population

Race	Percent of Felony Defendants	Percent of Detained Defendants
Black	79.8	83.4
Latino	13.9	11.2
White	6.4	5.4

even when compared to defendants of the same age, facing the same charges, and with the same type of counsel.[10]

Perhaps even more noteworthy is that fact that, while being Black is the strongest predictor of being detained pretrial (as shown in Table 2.4), defendants' race has no statistically significant relationship to a defendant's case outcome. Instead, as Table 2.5 shows, pretrial detention status is the greatest predictor of whether or not a defendant will be convicted. Controlling for race, age, legal representation, and offense, individuals who are detained pending adjudication have odds of being convicted that are 2.188 times greater than individuals who are released.

Table 2.4 Black defendants have greater odds of being detained than other defendants

Variable	Odds Ratio	SE
Black	1.580★★★	0.103
Age	1.068★★	0.024
Age squared	.999★	0
Public Defender	1.321★	0.119
Number of Drug Charges	0.974	0.035
Number of Weapons Charges	0.982	0.032
Number of Property Charges	0.954	0.049
Number of Violent Charges	1.168★★★	0.032
Constant	.153★★★	0.409
★ p < .05	★★★ p <.001	

Table 2.5 Pretrial Detention status is the greatest predictor of defendants' case outcomes

Variable	Odds Ratio	SE
Black	1.289	0.139
Age	1.043	0.034
Age squared	0.999	0
Public Defender	1.779★★	0.203
Drug Charges	1.219★★	0.063
Weapons Charges	1.105	0.04
Property Charges	1.937★★★	0.169
Violent Charges	1.026	0.036
Detained	2.188★★★	0.125
Constant	2.226	0.564
★ p < .05	★★ p < .01	★★★ p <.001

Taken together, this means that even absent a race-*based* disparity in case outcomes, there is still an actual racial disparity in case outcomes. In Cook County—as in criminal justice systems across the country—pretrial detention is a critical mechanism through which the already pervasive racial disparities in the criminal justice system are further entrenched and Black defendants are further disadvantaged.

Notes

1 Phrase taken from a discussion about the relationship between pretrial detention and plea deals in Foote (1965a).
2 See Appendix for more details on this and other quantitative analyses.
3 All names have been changed in the interest of confidentiality per Human Subjects guidelines by the IRB.
4 Petersen (2019a) argues that this is particularly true in "counties characterized by higher caseloads, fewer prosecutorial resources, and less jail capacity" (p. 1027).
5 While the concept of the courtroom workgroup has been largely accepted as an accurate description of how courtroom actors work together to process criminal cases, the simplicity of this concept does belie the extensive bodies of research on each of the primary courtroom actors, on the relationships between them, and on the rise of plea bargaining in the American criminal justice system. Moreover, many public defenders note that prosecutors' disproportionate leverage and the trial penalty mean that plea bargains often are the best outcomes for their clients (see, for example, Jones et al. (2018), referenced above). The point here is not to either simplify or summarize any of these debates, but rather to use this concept as a framework for thinking about defendants' experiences with the court process.
6 In addition to highlighting the common experience of a defendant being encouraged to plead guilty by his or her public defender, Brandon's comment also speaks to a common pattern among Black men I interviewed, who regularly spoke about their experiences in terms of "we" and "us," rather than or in addition to "me" and "I." This pattern is discussed further later in this chapter.
7 The fact that Foote's typology continues to be the most comprehensive framework for explaining why pretrial detentions facilitated poor case outcomes speaks directly to the need for more qualitative research on pretrial detention. Absent this work, researchers can document these outcomes and can hypothesize as to their causal power, but cannot test these hypotheses or document and analyze the processes by which the outcomes occur.
8 The bullpen is the common nickname for the various holding cells where detained defendants were held when being transferred into and out of the jail and the courthouse.
9 In order to address this challenge, some public defenders' offices do accept collect calls. There is no data on how many public defenders'

offices do and do not accept collect calls, but there is no standard expectation that they do so.

10 This dataset did not allow me to control for criminal history, which in most research is highly correlated with both being Black and being detained pretrial. Per Omori and Petersen (2020), given what we know about race and policing, using criminal history as an ostensibly race neutral factor undoubtedly allows for substantial underestimation of racial disparities in criminal justice outcomes and should be considered a way of institutionalizing racial inequality.

3 "But What Will Become Of The Innocent?"[1]

Of the dozens of people I interviewed as part of this research, two are seared into my memory beyond all others, two individuals who were never convicted of any crimes, but whose detentions left indelible scars. Calvin and Aaron were both arrested for crimes they did not commit, both were formally charged with those crimes, and both spent time in jail because they could not afford to pay bail. Ultimately, both were released from custody absent a finding of guilt, Calvin because the prosecutor dismissed all charges in a *nolle prosequi*, or "decline to prosecute," and Aaron because he was acquitted at a bench trial. Their experiences, described below, provide a window into one of the most disturbing—and yet often ignored—aspects of pretrial detention: the incarceration of those individuals who are never convicted of a crime.

Calvin

I interviewed Calvin at the South Shore Cultural Center, a historic landmark operated by the Chicago Park District on the southeast side of the city, right along the shore of Lake Michigan. Calvin and I had agreed to meet on the second floor of the Cultural Center/ Fieldhouse in one of the classrooms that are used for clubs, after-school programs, and the like. The first thing that stood out to me when Calvin walked into the room was his size: Calvin was at least a full foot taller than my 5 feet, 4 inches, and not in a long, lanky kind of way; Calvin was a big guy. The second thing that stood out was the packet of papers he held. "I brought these to show you," he told me, handing me the packet before we even introduced ourselves or sat down to begin our conversation. Looking down at the papers in my hand, I quickly recognized them as a State of Illinois Record of Arrests and Prosecutions, more commonly known as a "RAP sheet." As we sat down, Calvin told me that he had been arrested five times in his life, and held in jail on three of those occasions. Every time, the charges had been dismissed in anywhere from a few days to a few weeks. Despite Calvin never having been convicted of a crime, it was clear that these experiences had had a lasting effect on his life. From his perspective, everything began when he was arrested for the first time, about six years earlier.

Calvin had recently been discharged from the Army and had walked to a local convenience store with some friends to pick up beer on a Saturday afternoon. Unbeknownst to them, Chicago was in the midst of an overdose epidemic tied to fentanyl-laced heroin, and the Chicago Police Department (CPD) was on high alert. Walking out of the convenience store holding a 40 oz bottle of beer, Calvin greeted a couple of men who were standing outside the store dealing drugs. "I knew them and I knew what they was doing, but that wasn't part of my life," Calvin noted, pointing out that the guys selling the heroin were from his neighborhood and that he had not seen them since being discharged from the army a few weeks prior. Nonetheless, the conversation appeared incriminating and a few minutes later when a group of officers swooped in to arrest them, Calvin was cuffed too. "[The officer] saw me coming from the store and I had a 40-ounce beer, it wasn't open yet. He… grabbed me and arrested me. That's how I got my first case, right there… that's my first trip going [to jail]. It was just like 'wow!' I just got out the Army and I wasn't dealing heroin."

Calvin was taken down to the local police station and then transported to the courthouse, where he was placed in a holding cell with several dozen other men who had been arrested in the past 24 hours. Although he assumed that he was being arrested for dealing drugs based on conversations he overheard from the officers who arrested him and those at the police station, Calvin did not learn what he was being charged with until he appeared before a judge at bond court almost 12 hours later. Appearing before the judge, next to a public defender he had never spoken with before, Calvin learned that he was being charged with attempted murder, as the heroin that he had not been involved in distributing was being connected to a series of fentanyl-related overdose deaths around the city.

The bond hearing was a blur, lasting no more than 30 seconds, and at the end, the judge set bail at $320,000. In Illinois's Deposit bond, or "D-bond," system, this meant that Calvin would need to come up with $32,000 to obtain his release. He was placed back in the "bullpen" with the other defendants and, at the end of the bond court session, transported to the jail through the underground complex that links Cook County's Criminal Courthouse with its jail. When he finally got access to a phone several hours later, Calvin made collect calls to his girlfriend and his mother to tell them what had happened and to try to allay their concerns about his sudden disappearance the day before. There was no discussion of trying to find $32,000 to bail him out, so he began the waiting process, mentally preparing to exonerate himself at his next court hearing.

The preparation turned out to be unnecessary. Exactly six weeks later, having had no contact with the public defender's office and no further information about his case, Calvin was brought from the jail to his arraignment hearing and told that the prosecution was dismissing the charge. Again, the court process occurred so quickly, that Calvin barely understood what happened; it was not until several years later when he learned that he could request his RAP sheet that he saw that he had been *"nolle'd,"* when the state's attorney's office had declined to pursue charges. As he described it: "No sentence, whatever that means [pointing to the words *Nolle Prosequi* on his RAP sheet]… I don't even know what that means. They just threw it off."

Given the seriousness of the charge—attempted murder—one can only assume that the prosecution did not make the *nolle prosequi* decision because the charge was not worth pursuing, but rather that they lacked evidence to support this charge in court—nevermind any less serious drug distribution charges. After telling the judge that Calvin was too dangerous to be out on the streets and requesting a bail amount to demonstrate this, the prosecution implicitly acknowledged its mistake, by *nolle'ing* all charges. This done, the judge ordered Calvin released, the Sheriff's Office complied, and Calvin was a free man. Of course, no one ever apologized to Calvin, nor did anyone ever give him any kind of explanation for what happened. Moreover, no one could take back the trauma that he had experienced over those six weeks, or the ways in which that experience framed much of his life in the following years. But more on that later.

Aaron

In contrast to Calvin, who has been arrested several times but never convicted of a crime, Aaron did end up being convicted of a felony, about a year after being accused of the crime for which he was detained pretrial and, after nine months in custody, acquitted. At the time of our interview, Aaron was on felony probation for a drug-related charge, and we met in an office at the Cook County Adult Probation Department. Aaron was 18 at the time of our interview and 17 at the time of the arrest that would result in nine months in Cook County Jail before being acquitted at a bench trial.

Growing up in a low-income Black neighborhood on the South Side of Chicago, he had long seen police in his neighborhood and knew a number of people, including those his age or younger, who had been arrested before. Aaron's first personal experience with the criminal justice system occurred when he was 17. He was hanging out with a couple of friends after school one afternoon, cruising around the neighborhood in a friend's car, when police siren and lights went on and the group was pulled over. Ordering everyone out and searching the car, the officers quickly found what they had been looking for: an expensive jacket that had been forcibly taken from another teenager in the neighborhood earlier that afternoon. The young man's mother had called the police and CPD had been looking for the car that Aaron was in.

Aaron and his friends were arrested on the spot and taken to the police station where they were booked for armed robbery and, because 17-year-olds who are accused of felonies are considered adults in Illinois's justice system, transported to the Cook County Criminal Court to face criminal charges. At bond court the following morning Aaron met briefly with a public defender who asked a short list of questions that might affect bond determination—prior criminal history, ties to the community, education or employment status— and then he appeared before the judge. At the end of a bond hearing that was even shorter than Aaron's meeting with the public defender, the judge made his decision: $30,000 "D," or $3,000 deposit to obtain release. By almost all objective measures, a more lenient bail determination would have been appropriate: although robbery is a class two felony, Aaron posed neither a danger to the community nor a high flight risk. He had no prior criminal record; as a teenager who lived at home, attended school regularly, and had lived in the same neighborhood his whole life, he was unlikely to abscond; in addition, he had no income of his own and came from a poor family.

When I asked Aaron what he thought when he learned that he could get out for $3,000, he told me, "It was like no thought behind it because, like, me staying in a household with my mother, it's already a struggle for her to come up with what she has for the rent once a month. I'm like wow, there's no thought that I'm going to leave here. It's either I'm in the cell for a long time or until the truth come out."

"The truth," that Aaron referred to was simple and uncontested by anyone involved in the jacket robbery: Aaron had not participated in any way, was not with the other young men at the time, and had no way of knowing what they had done. Upon being arrested, Aaron's friends vouched for him, telling CPD that he had not been involved even while acknowledging that they had. The victim, too, told the police and later the prosecutor that he had been robbed by three teenagers and that Aaron was not one of them.

When Aaron finally got in touch with his mother and told her what had happened, she was adamant that he not plead guilty to something he hadn't done. Concerned that the public defender would not take the case to trial, Aaron's mom reached out to his uncle, who agreed to pay for a private attorney. Nine months after his arrest, a few months after his 18th birthday, Aaron was tried in front of a judge at a bench trial. The young men he had been in the car with, who had since plead guilty, and the young man who was robbed of his jacket, all testified that he had had nothing to do with the robbery. The judge found Aaron not guilty and he was released. I asked Aaron how he felt when the judge declared him not guilty.

> To me, it was like, I wish instead of taking nine months that it did that it could have been a lot more sooner than it was, you know. Just so what was said out of my mouth about what I know that I did—nine months, you see something different after nine months compared to what was being said at day one?

In addition, as with Calvin, Aaron's life was indelibly marked by his detention, regardless of the fact that he was acquitted. I discuss that further below.

Pretrial Detention, Innocence, and Punishment

The title of this chapter, "But what will become of the innocent?", comes from Supreme Court Justice Thurgood Marshall's dissenting opinion in *US v. Salerno* (1987), in which the majority upheld the constitutionality of the expansion of preventive detention[2] legislated in the 1984 Bail Reform Act. In response to the plaintiff's contention that by depriving defendants of liberty before trial, preventive detentions violated Fifth Amendment due process guarantees, the majority ruled that because the intent of preventive detention was regulatory rather than punitive, it did not violate the Fifth Amendment. Justice Marshall adamantly disagreed with this reasoning, arguing that the punitive effect of pretrial preventive detention made irrelevant any regulatory intent. Moreover, he noted that if it was unconstitutional to detain a defendant after he was acquitted, it could not logically be acceptable to detain this same defendant prior to trial, unless the presumption of innocence was disregarded; if innocence required freedom from incarceration, the presumption of innocence surely required the same (Eason, 1988).

These two issues—the presumption of innocence and punishment before trial—have long been central concerns for scholars and policymakers addressing the pretrial detentions of defendants who are not found guilty. The Supreme Court has debated the meaning of the presumption of innocence for centuries, with some justices arguing that this principle is merely a procedural directive regarding the treatment of the accused at trial while others have argued, like Justice Marshall, that the presumption of innocence requires accused defendants to be treated in all ways like innocent people. In the aforementioned decision for *US v. Salerno*, the majority took the former view, arguing, "the presumption of innocence 'allocates the burden of proof in criminal trials… but it has no application to a determination of the rights of a pretrial detainee during confinement before his trial.'" By contrast, in a dissent written eight years before *US v. Salerno*, Justice Stevens argued "that the presumption 'shield[s] a person awaiting trial from potentially oppressive governmental actions' by presuming 'both that he is innocent of prior criminal conduct and that he has no present intention to commit any offense'" (Eason 1988: 1072).

Others writing on the topic have addressed it from a less abstract perspective, drawing on empirical experience to argue for the punitiveness of pretrial detention. Jeff Thaler (1978), an attorney with the criminal appeals bureau of the Legal Aid Society, wrote that for his clients the ubiquity of pretrial detentions made into a "myth" the notion that a defendant is presumed innocent until proven guilty. In reality, he argued, "a person's presumed innocence is overcome by an arrest or indictment" as well as by "a bail proceeding where a magistrate uses the severity of the unproven offense to predict whether, if released, the accused will flee or commit a crime" (p. 441). Like Foote before him and Justice Marshall after him, Thaler pointed to the punitive nature of pretrial detention as evidence of the contradiction between the presumption of innocence and the pretrial incarceration of the accused, arguing, like Justice Marshall, that the punitive effect of pretrial detentions made irrelevant the lack of punitive intent. "While there may be no 'intent' to punish, pretrial detention, even with the 'least necessary restraint,' has consequences (social, psychological, economic, and legal) which are felt as punishment by the accused and may be seen as punishment by society" (p. 451). Detailing the punitive effects of pretrial detentions, regardless of detainees' ultimate criminal justice outcomes, Thaler raised the same issues as did Foote (1954, 1958a and b, 1959) and Brockett (1971): pretrial detentions entail physical discomfort and deprivation, isolation from family and loved ones, job loss and other economic hardships, to name the most important. In addition, Thaler pointed out that being acquitted and having charges dismissed does not necessarily alleviate the stigma of incarceration, and former detainees may suffer reputational damage even if they are not convicted.

Miller and Guggenheim (1990) raise the same issues. Analyzing normative social and legal conceptions of "the essential notion of punishment," they argue that even a cursory assessment of the effects of pretrial detentions evidences their punitiveness (p. 342). The importance of determining the punitive effect of pretrial detentions notwithstanding, however, they also argue that pretrial detentions are punitive in a more fundamental sense, regardless of their consequences for people's lives: pointing out that "imprisonment is the modern norm of punishment," they argue that imprisonment for any reason cannot be stripped of its inherent punitiveness: stated directly, the "nature of detention [is] rarely benign from any perspective" (pp. 368–369).

Presumption of Innocence

Unsurprisingly, neither Calvin nor Aaron perceived a presumption of innocence during the course of his detention. Similar to the individuals discussed in Chapter 2, both Calvin and Aaron noted that they were treated as if guilty from the moment they were arrested. As Aaron recalled, despite knowing that he had done nothing wrong, the way he was treated at the point of arrest convinced him that he would be found guilty. "It was like, the officers, as I was being arrested, one of the officers was telling me what the charges was, how much time that it carries. I'm like man, that's where I'm going to be." Calvin concurred: "I guess as soon as you get arrested all of your rights are gone out the door." Bringing up a similar point later in our interview, Calvin again pointed to the experience of the criminal justice system and the actions of the criminal justice system actors as demonstrating their presumption of his guilt: "Just being in the County [jail], the way they treat you like you already convicted. Like they already got your clothes ready for you to go down [to the penitentiary]."

Similar to the individuals in Chapter 2 who ultimately did plead guilty, for the individuals discussed in this chapter—both legally and factually innocent—it is a cumulative series of encounters with criminal justice processes that cements the realization that they are presumed guilty. Notwithstanding the Supreme Court's determination of the presumption of innocence as a procedural directive regarding the treatment of defendants at trial, their experiences and those of other individuals who are never convicted belie this axiom as it is more colloquially understood. Moreover, the fact that the vast majority of defendants never go to trial underscores the disjuncture between the Supreme Court's interpretation of the presumption of innocence and defendants' experience thereof. As discussed below, the experiences of individuals charged with two types of crimes particularly exemplify this contradiction: drug possession and domestic violence.

"It was Zero Point Zero Zero Percent of Drugs"

One of the most common reasons why defendants spend time in jail before having their charges dismissed is because they are awaiting results from the drug lab. According to Richard Devine, who was the Cook County State's Attorney from 1996 through 2008, approximately 30 percent of drug cases in Cook County are dismissed upon completion of lab results. Nonetheless, because bail determinations are based primarily on charges, defendants often sit in jail in the meantime. Moreover, although lab results are supposed to be completed within a couple of days of arrest, in Cook County—as in many jurisdictions around the country—the lab is overworked and under-funded and results routinely take four–six weeks to be completed. The experiences of Sam and Nicole, described below, provide a window into this experience for innocent defendants.

Sam, a White man in his mid-30s, spent a month and a half in jail awaiting lab results. He was pulled over on a routine traffic stop and arrested for PCS when the police officer mistook a bag of laundry detergent for cocaine.

> I had a box of detergent and some detergent in a zip lock bag with soap and washing supplies, bleach for laundry. They took the Ziploc bag and assumed it was cocaine. Even though it was written on there, "soap"—it had all the soap and washing products right there. I couldn't pay $6,600 to get out. I was very frustrated. One, I knew that I didn't have any cocaine.

> The police officers didn't listen to me, didn't believe me. They jumped a leap there with looking at a bunch of bleach and washing detergent and then assume it's cocaine when one could see with the blue little crystals in the soap, it didn't look like what they ought to know cocaine looks like and smells like... it was unjust and I was presumed guilty...

Legally, the presumption of innocence means that if Sam had gone to trial, the judge and jury would have to presume his innocence and the prosecution prove his guilt "beyond a reasonable doubt." Practically speaking, however, Sam was treated as guilty at every step of the way. First, the police "jumped a leap" and assumed his laundry supplies were drugs. At court, the prosecution assumed the police's interpretation to be correct and filed criminal charges for possession of a controlled substance (PCS). Based on the type and volume of drugs Sam was alleged to have possessed—a large Ziploc bag, filled with cocaine—the judge set his bail at $66,000 "D," requiring a $6,600 deposit bond to get out. Unable to afford bond, Sam had no choice but to stay in custody until his next court date, the preliminary hearing, which the judge scheduled for 39 days later. When Sam finally returned to court after almost six weeks in jail, the lab report had not arrived. At the assent of the prosecution and the defense, the judge was about to issue a continuance, sending Sam back to jail for another month. Desperate and feeling like he had nothing to lose, Sam spoke up.

> I was in court and the judge said, "was the lab back?" [and the prosecutor said] no. I grabbed the public defender and I said, "look, I told them, this was for washing my clothes. Please ask them to call the lab right now. It's been 40 days. Can you please call them?" He asked the judge if I could speak. I told the judge and the judge said "if you're lying, I'm going to slam you when it comes back." I said "I'm not lying to you." The judge called back. Made me go in the back and wait about another 30 minutes. Finally, I came back in and they realized it was laundry soap.
> Author: They dismissed the charges?
> Yes. [I was] very, you know, upset, angry, I felt like the system didn't work for me. I understood if I did something wrong. Or if there was even suspicion. I was pulled over on a traffic stop and I had a box of laundry supplies.[3]

Nicole's experience largely echoed Sam's. A Black woman in her mid-50s, Nicole had never had a run in with the criminal justice

system before being pulled over for a routine traffic violation and arrested for possession of a controlled substance. Like Sam, she waited
almost six weeks before lab results confirmed that a vial of liquid in
her car was not PCP, although unlike Sam, she was only detained for
ten days before she was able to borrow money for bail. For Nicole,
the ordeal began when she was pulled over for running a red light
and, in what was perhaps the unlikeliest of errors, the police officer
arrested her when he mistook a vial of holy oil for PCP.

> He stopped me up in like an alley. I had to get out of the car.
> He wanted to search the car and search me. My daughter was
> with me. He did all of that and then he came back and said,
> "yeah, we found drugs." Why would I ask him to search ev-
> erything if I had drugs! It was not looking good. But the drugs
> he thought he had found was holy oil that my daddy had given
> me. [The police officer] said it was PCP. I said no. If it was like
> marijuana or something—but PCP? I'm scared of that! I said
> "open it up and smell it." He's like, "no because if I touch it, it
> will be on my hands." He acted like it was acid. So of course,
> they locked me up. They put handcuffs on me. I'm like oh this
> is not comfortable!

Nicole's car was impounded and she and her 14-year-old daughter
were taken down to the police station where the police officer let
Nicole call a friend to pick up her daughter before booking her on
PCS charges.

> They took my car. I'm like, oh my goodness! There's too much
> going on. I'm brand new to this whole thing. I don't know what
> to do or say. You say one wrong thing. I didn't say much of
> nothing because I was just amazed. I didn't want to go to jail.
> I had to spend the night [at the police station]. After that it got
> worse. Just worse, worse, worse.

When Nicole got to court, her bail was set at $9,000 "D," requiring
a $900 deposit bond to get out. Fortunately for Nicole, after ten
days in detention, her pastor was able to lend her enough money to
get out on bail. By that time, the cost of getting her car out of the
city pound was another $800. "My pastor gave me $900 to get me
out because I was working [at the church] then. By the time I got
through it was income tax time. My car was $800 to get out. I'm like
oh, this is a lot!"

Nicole went to court for her preliminary hearing only to have the judge continue her case because the lab results were not in. Finally, a month after being released from jail and six weeks after being arrested, the lab results came back and she was cleared.

> I went down there and when they finally called my case, the judge called me up there and he read off all the charges and stuff. He said let's get to the drug thing. I couldn't wait for him to get to it because it wasn't drugs. The judge said, "it was zero point zero zero percent of drugs." Most of the court laughed. The police is thinking I'm going down. It was just a moment. [The judge said] "You supposed to have been in traffic court." [I told him,] "I tried to tell everybody and nobody wanted to hear me." The judge laughed a little. Then he let me finish it off with traffic court. I went to traffic court and I paid some fines and then it was a wrap.

Although the bond money Nicole had borrowed from her pastor was refunded after the charges were dismissed, the $800 she had paid to get her car out of the pound was not recoverable, even though the charges upon which the impoundment had been predicated were proven false. Like Sam, Nicole's experience made her mad:

> Actually, to tell you the truth after I went through all that, I hated police for a minute, I just hated them. I wasn't no lawbreaker. The fact that they can get what they want and do what they want. It was just not, I'm thinking about all the other folks in there. Most of them aren't real criminals. The REAL criminals y'all ain't caught. You wasting my time.

"I wasn't Guilty, I was Innocent. Three Weeks Wasted of My Life."

Domestic violence charges were one of the most common reasons why the individuals I interviewed were arrested and detained, and one for which many insisted on their innocence. Domestic violence is, of course, a notoriously difficult offense to prove and one for which prosecutions are rare, which means that the rate of incidence is undoubtedly much higher than the rate of criminal prosecution and conviction. At the same time, there is evidence to suggest that the shift toward greater enforcement of domestic violence laws over the last 40 years has—like much criminal justice enforcement—ensnared innocent people. Here, too, bail determinations based on charges mean that innocent individuals spend time in jail often with little evidence.

Beginning in the 1970s, jurisdictions across the United States began changing their approach to domestic violence, shifting from a paradigm that treated intimate partner violence as a private matter to one that recognized it as a criminal act. As part of this shift, law enforcement agencies were increasingly encouraged to arrest alleged perpetrators—often through "mandatory arrest" laws or "preferred arrest" laws that require or encourage law enforcement officers to make an arrest whenever there is probable cause to believe that domestic violence may have occurred (Hirschel et al. 2007). Even in states like Illinois, where there is not a statutory mandate to make an arrest in these cases, both law and policy strongly encourage law enforcement officers to do so. For 22-year-old Marlon, this meant three weeks in jail following an argument with a neighbor.

Offended that Marlon had not invited her to a party he was having, Marlon's neighbor came over to interrupt the party and give Marlon a piece of her mind. The argument soon became heated and, when the neighbors called the police, Marlon's uninvited neighbor told the responding officers that he had "put his hands on her." Despite the fact that no witnesses supported this accusation, the officers arrested Marlon for battery, a misdemeanor. At bond court the following morning, Marlon's bail was set at $25,000 "D," requiring a $2,500 deposit bond for release. As with the experiences of other respondents, nothing about the process felt fair to Marlon, nor did he feel like he was presumed innocent.

> You don't get to talk to the judge or try to plead your case. You talk to these public defenders basically and they tell you, well they ask you a lot of questions, you know. Things that they can tell the judge that make your case better so you can get a lower bond. I told my public defender basically that I was in school, I had a son, I had a job interview the next day, and everything. So, I guess that they take that to the judge and the judge looks it over or whatever, and they set your bond. I got a high bond and no one could pay to get me out so I had to stay in jail...

Three weeks later, when Marlon's neighbor did not show up to testify at his preliminary hearing, the judge dismissed the charges and Marlon was released. When I interviewed him only a few weeks later, Marlon was still in shock. "I had a domestic charge—a domestic violence charge! And basically, off of somebody's word I was taken to jail and I felt like that was unfair... I'm 22. I just got my first speeding ticket. It's just, it's wild."

As with Calvin, Aaron, Sam, and Nicole, the way that Marlon describes his experience shows how being taken to jail made it clear to him that he was never presumed innocent. Moreover, despite the legalistic hair-splitting that separates the meaning of the presumption of innocence from the question of whether pretrial detention constitutes punishment, these respondents and their experiences also evidence the many ways in which their detentions harmed them, functioning as actual punishment, even if not legal punishment. Below, I discuss the punitive detention experiences of these innocent individuals.

Punishment Before Trial

In an analysis of the Supreme Court's ruling in *US v. Salerno*, law professors Marc Miller and Martin Guggenheim (1990) critiqued the majority's declaration that preventive detention does not constitute punishment, pointing out that case law has long recognized both "the punisher's intent" and "the effects suffered by the punished individual" as considerations in defining punishment (p. 365). Miller and Guggenheim note that, despite a somewhat lengthy body of case law on what does and does not constitute punishment, there is no constitutional definition of punishment. Concerned about this gap given the Court's *Salerno* ruling, Miller and Guggenheim propose one, arguing:

> To be constitutional a deprivation must: (1) involve a restraint on liberty or property otherwise enjoyed by a free citizen; (2) *not* be justified by a clear, substantial, nonpunitive purpose; (3) be imposed by the authorized and legitimate legal authority; and (4) be imposed based on a final adjudication finding a violation of a law, or specific anticipated violation of a law, with scienter. (p. 370; italics original)

Parsing this further, they argue, "If a deprivation is not justified by such a nonpunitive purpose and it appears to be based on a violation of law but without that finding following a trial, then courts should disallow it as unconstitutional punishment" (p. 371). Miller and Guggenheim's proposal was, of course, largely an intellectual exercise; while there is no comprehensive legal definition of punishment, the *Salerno* ruling stands and pretrial detention, legally, is not punishment. Case law and semantic debates notwithstanding, the way in which individuals who are detained pretrial describe their experiences makes clear that they view it as a form of punishment.

"Imprisonment is the Modern Norm of Punishment"

As (dissenting) Supreme Court justices, lawyers, and researchers have noted, the fact that imprisonment is the normative form of state sanctioned punishment in our society fundamentally undermines any attempts to decouple incarceration and punishment. Certainly, the way legally innocent former detainees describe their time in custody validates the argument, as respondents regularly demonstrate the synonymity of detention and imprisonment, both through the specific language they use to talk about their time in detention and in the ways in which they describe that experience.

When describing his time in custody, Aaron repeatedly conveys a lack of differentiation between his detention and incarceration as punishment for a crime, referring to himself as having "done nine months" at multiple points in our conversation. Asked at the end of our interview to reflect on his experience, the language he uses shows the indistinguishability between pretrial detention and intentionally punitive forms of incarceration in his mind, and his description of the experience demonstrates why.

> I say incarceration is not worth it. It ain't. There ain't no excitement in there. It's a lot that go on in there. A lot of people would never think what goes on if you never been there. A person that's been locked up been through a lot more than another person would think about being locked up for a certain time it ain't too much. But, you know, sometimes you gotta think about being locked up for a certain time, you got a lot of time, being with a lot of different attitudes. Not just the inmates. The officers and, you know, a lot of different attitudes that you around, then the stressful cause you going through.
>
> You don't have no, you don't have no walls, no door to walk out, to walk this thing, to walk that thing. You just get a thought in your head that's the only way, you know, you can relieve any type of stress. You can't get a clear thought.

This description of his detention, with its focus on being trapped, was one that Aaron brought up repeatedly throughout the course of our discussion:

> It's like so much stuff you try to avoid being locked up but you really can't because you just stuck. You know, it ain't like you can walk around the corner or walk to the store, you just stuck.

You wake up the same person with the same problems, the same thing went on the next day. Being locked up, it ain't, I don't think it's for nobody.

More than anything, he noted, the total deprivation of freedom and complete lack of control over his own life—the very characteristics that define incarceration as a form of punishment—were the most difficult aspects of his detention.

> It's, like, really having to be told what to do. It's not even like what you're being told to do, like you know just something out-rageous, but just having to totally say well, "you all says, such and such." That ain't something I feel I can keep living life going through.

Calvin's descriptions of his time in detention also echoes Aaron's, both in his conflation between detention and imprisonment, as he refers to other—also unconvicted—detained individuals as prison-ers, and in his focus on being trapped and having no choices.

> Demeaning. First, it's like you not, you not anything. In other words, you're just a piece of meat. "Get in there and do this." It's just you gotta have a lot of strong will when you get up in there. The first thing you can't show weakness and they sense, the guards and the other prisoners, you gotta go in there with a strong men-tality... It's basically just, I guess it's just a part of you being in there. They say "well you in here, you deserve to get treated like this."

Nicole, recalling conversations she had while detained with women who had been to prison before, put it succinctly: "Locked up is locked up. I just need to be free."

"My Mom was Really, Like, Going Through the Worries."

As Thaler noted, "While there may be no 'intent' to punish, pretrial detention, even with the 'least necessary restraint' has consequences (social, psychological, economic, and legal) which are felt as pun-ishment by the accused and may be seen as punishment by society" (1978: 451; also cited above). This, too, is validated by the experi-ences of the individuals I interviewed.

For Aaron, the hardest part was balancing his own loneliness with his desire not to burden his already struggling family. Knowing that his mother did not have the financial resources to pay for collect calls from the jail or to contribute funds for the commissary, Aaron, at 17, did his best to ask for nothing.

> I'm really just trying to go through it like basically by myself. Me knowing that my mom had the house problems with the bills—she got seven kids including me, so that's six in her household that gotta be tooken care of. When it came to commissary, you know, it weren't really too much I could get at the commissary. I rather for her not to send no money to me, just spend it on the household and my sisters and brothers.

Despite his loneliness, he also discouraged his family from visiting, partially to protect himself from the difficulty of seeing them leave and partially to protect himself from seeing how devastating this detention was for them. "[My mom] was really, like, going through the worries... Then for me to know that she was going to go through worries, I really didn't want to communicate with her, what she knowing I was gonna be at... my mom would come to see me, she be crying." Despite his best efforts to shield himself, it was clear that being in custody took a toll on Aaron. Two months after he was found not guilty and released from jail, Aaron was arrested again, this time for drug possession. After spending nine months in custody fighting the charges the first time he was arrested, he had learned his lesson and decided to plead guilty right away.

> I was only out exactly two months, I was out two months from doing nine months when I caught the drug case... I thought "I want to be outside. I am going take anything today to get off this hopefully."

Despite the fact that Aaron was found not guilty of the charge that lead to his nine-month pretrial detention, his time in custody still caused irreparable harm and, in some sense, did lead to an eventual guilty plea and conviction.

Calvin, by contrast, had never been convicted of any crime when I interviewed him six years after his detention. Nonetheless, he made clear the damage wrought both during and in the aftermath of his detention. Unsurprisingly, Calvin's detention was hard on his family, who knew that he was innocent but still worried that he might be convicted. "It took a toll on my mother especially when she knew I didn't do anything like that. Because they know the type of person I am. I'm big and burly, but I'm not the type just to go out there and start anything… It hurts them just to see me go through that stuff and I hate to have to hurt them like that." The stress took an even heavier toll on Calvin's girlfriend, who was pregnant at the time. Shortly after he was released, she miscarried; to Calvin and her, it was clear that the stress of his detention and the surrounding uncertainty was the primary cause of the miscarriage. Not long after his release, they broke up, the combined stress of his detention and the miscarriage being more than they could handle.

> My first girlfriend, she—when I got arrested and had to do the time—she, it worried her so much she had a miscarriage. So, you know, it strained on that relationship. Then we broke up after that but now I, I still talk to her… But I didn't want her to go through that and I didn't know she was pregnant but she was two months pregnant but then she came down [to the jail], I think like a week later after I got out, she had a miscarriage because of all the stress that was going on. It really affected her too.

Having just gotten home from the army, Calvin was not fully employed yet at the time of his detention, but had picked up some odd jobs working under the table for a friend who ran a moving company. She quickly restaffed him after his release, but what Calvin thought had been a temporary job to tide him over while he found something more formal became increasingly permanent as he found that, even without having been convicted, his arrest record was scaring off potential employers.

> After that, you know what I'm saying, I left, when I left the army after four years, after I got that arrest, a lot of stuff changed too because, you know what I'm saying, I missed job opportunities and by that being on my record, it's hard for me to get a job now.
> Author: Even though you weren't convicted?
> Just the arrest, it being on my record. Especially, I could beat up or stab or rob somebody but you got a heroin [charge], they either think I'm heroin addict or a dealer. And I was never either one of them. And so, I been trying since then, [but] I really never had a regular job.

Although most research examining the effect of criminal records on employment has focused on individuals with felony convictions, there is a small but growing body of research examining whether and to what extent lower level forms of criminal justice contact, like arrests, affect people's job attainment.[4] This work validates Calvin's experience, with a recent audit study showing that, while arrests do not affect employment as negatively as felony convictions do, they nonetheless do reduce the likelihood that an employer will contact a job applicant (Uggen et al. 2014). An older economics analysis analyzing the relationship between arrest and employment for Black versus White men found that arrests have a long-term effect on employment and account for almost one-third of the difference in employment outcomes for Black and White men (Grogger 1992). While this study did not differentiate between arrests that did and did not result in convictions, it is nonetheless compelling evidence of the effect of arrests on employment, especially for Black men. In testimony to the US Equal Opportunity Employment Commission, Amy Solomon, Senior Advisor to the Assistant Attorney General in the Office of Justice Programs at the US Department of Justice in the Obama Administration, corroborated the prevalence of this issue, talking at length about the inclusion of arrest records in criminal background checks, noting that while up to one-third of felony arrests do not lead to a conviction, arrested individuals nonetheless do have a criminal record that shows up on a background check (Solomon 2012).

Toward the end of my interview with Calvin, I asked him if he could sum up how he thought his experience with the criminal justice system had affected him. More than six years after his arrest and detention, it was clear that the impact was both deep and long-lasting, and that he was still struggling to come to terms with it:

> I would say, it made me more aware of the things that—my record is holding me back. But and it also showed me how people would rather judge you on a piece of paper before they get to know you from what you really you are. And so, I really don't know how much financially it really hurt because I hadn't gotten it yet to lose it, you got to have it to lose it, so I really don't know how that affected me. But I know I haven't showed the world my full potential. Because I know what I can do but it's not, it's a lot of people out there not giving me the chance of showing what I can do… Then I see it's on my record because I know they'll look at that paper first before they get to know me and then if the people take the chance and just say, let me try him out for two weeks to see how he really works… And I just wait. My time is gonna come and it's gonna show that I'm

a better person that I want to be, you know what I'm saying. A person for myself, a better person of myself is gonna come out and I'm just waiting on that time. I just, I know I got this record but someone out there is gonna take a chance on me and the rest of the world gonna see what they missed.

Notes

1 Marshall, Thurgood. Dissent in *US v. Salerno*. Marshall was quoting Justice White's decision for the majority in *Coffin v. United States* in 1895, the decision in which the Court established the presumption of innocence as "axiomatic and elementary" for persons accused of crimes. In asking, "what will become of the innocent?" Justice White was himself quoting an anecdote from Roman history in which Caesar and Delphidius debated the legal status of the accused (www.duhaime.org).
2 As discussed in Chapter 1, preventive detention is a particular form of pretrial detention whereby a defendant is held without bail because he/she is determined to be too dangerous to release. Nationally, preventive detention is far less common as a cause of pretrial detention than inability to pay bail and none of the individuals I interviewed were preventively detained.
3 It does not seem coincidental that one of the few White people I interviewed was also the only person to report being allowed to address the judge directly. It is likely that the race-based assumptions Van Cleeve (2016) details among judges and defense counsel in Cook County worked in Sam's favor.
4 Kohler-Hausmann (2018) also has an extensive discussion of how various forms of criminal justice record keeping, including dismissals, "mark" defendants and affect their lives.

4 "Someone Has to Pay a Price..."[1]

Throughout the last two chapters, a number of people hinted at the financial implications of their time in custody. Reggie, who pleaded guilty to drug charges after five months in custody despite maintaining his innocence, discussed the financial strains of his detention: unable to draw his unemployment while in jail, he suffered the dual consequences of losing out on this income and being forced to use his savings to cover rent and other essential expenses during that time. Compared to many other individuals whom I spoke with, Reggie was fortunate to have that cushion; nonetheless the financial costs were a clear burden above and beyond the experience of detention and eventual criminal conviction.

Unsurprisingly, those individuals who were not convicted experienced comparable financial losses. Nicole, who was charged with possession of a controlled substance when a police officer mistook a vial of holy oil for PCP, was driving at the time of her arrest, which meant that her car was impounded, per standard policy in Cook County and most other jurisdictions. By the time she came up with money for bail ten days later, she had also incurred $800 in impoundment fees. Despite the fact that the drug tests came back negative and charges against Nicole were dismissed, she had no recourse to recoup these fees.

In this chapter, I delve more deeply into these financial harms and other material losses. In contrast to the prior two chapters which distinguished between the experiences of individuals who pleaded guilty from those who were never convicted, in this chapter, I interweave the experiences of individuals who are ultimately determined to be legally guilty and those who are not, demonstrating the comparability of the negative material consequences of pretrial detention for all people regardless of legal or actual guilt or innocence. In so doing, my goal is twofold: first, by showing the similarity in outcomes for people who are legally guilty and those who are not, I build upon the critical body of scholarship that focuses on the collateral consequences of incarceration by highlighting the detrimental consequences of incarceration independent of having a felony conviction. To date, most research on the collateral consequences of incarceration has addressed the consequences of being incarcerated and of having a felony simultaneously, often assuming or implying that these two circumstances inevitably go hand in hand. As this book shows, however, many of the collateral consequences of being incarcerated have nothing to do with being convicted of a felony; indeed, in many ways the material consequences of pretrial detention are equally damaging to those individuals who are not convicted as to those who are.

Second, in this chapter, I build on the argument made in the prior chapters regarding the divergence between the presumption of innocence as legally defined and the lived experience of guilt and innocence. The previous chapter showed how the intrinsic punitiveness of detention belies the notion that people are presumed innocent in the criminal legal process; this chapter further underscores the punitive nature of pretrial detention by showing the material harms detention causes for detained individuals and their families both during and after their time in custody, regardless of guilt.

Collateral Consequences of Incarceration

The negative economic consequences are probably the most-well documented of the "collateral consequences" of incarceration, with an extensive body of legal and policy research documenting an array of financially impactful consequences of having a felony conviction and a sizeable body of scholarship underscoring the difficulties people experience in securing employment following a felony conviction. In 2012, the American Bar Association (ABA) launched the National Inventory of the Collateral Consequences of Conviction (NICCC),[2] an interactive database that provides an extensive compendium of consequences of felony convictions in all 50 states and the federal system, including occupational and professional licensing; fines and fees; government benefits, loans, and grants; and more.

In addition to these "direct" collateral consequences, scholarship has demonstrated an array of indirect collateral consequences. Audit studies have long found employer discrimination against job applicants with felony convictions, with recent scholarship highlighting even worse outcomes for Black job applicants (Boshier and Johnson 1974; Buikhuisen and Dijksterhuis 1971; Pager 2003, 2007; Pager and Quillian 2005; Schwartz and Skolnick 1962). In addition, scholars working in the human and social capital paradigm have shown that incarceration reduces individuals' human capital by "undermin[ing] the acquisition of job skills among ex-inmates in comparison to others who remain continuously employed" (Western et al. 2001: 414; see also Waldfogel 1994). This, in turn, may limit former felons' opportunities for occupational mobility and wage growth by forcing them into low-skill jobs with low wages and few opportunities for advancement. In addition, by limiting incarcerated people's contact with social networks on the outside, incarceration reduces people's social capital, further constraining their opportunities for employment, especially more competitive or higher skill employment with growth opportunities (Western 2002; Western et al. 2000).

Even as we consider—and seek to remediate—the extensive, unnecessary, and counterproductive financial consequences of felony convictions, it is important not to stop there. Increasingly, researchers, advocates, and policymakers are recognizing that all forms of criminal justice system contact can have high economic costs.[3] Below, I discuss the direct and indirect material costs of pretrial detention, including job loss; material losses, such as cars, housing, and more; and opportunity costs.

"By Me Being in Jail that Long, You Know, I Lost the Job"

Not surprisingly, people who are detained for more than a couple of days almost always lose their jobs. The actual reason for termination differs from person to person: some people are terminated because they are unable or choose not to contact their employers from jail and are fired for missing work, while others do get in touch with their employers only to be terminated when their detentions carry on for longer than their employers can wait.

Thomas, who I introduced in Chapter 2, is one of the former. A Black man in his mid-50s who was struggling with addiction, Thomas was working as a manager at a car maintenance franchise when he was arrested for forgery. He had a couple of prior theft convictions related to his addiction and considered himself fortunate to have been able to find an employer who would take a chance on him despite his criminal record.

After his most recent arrest, Thomas was taken to the police station where he was booked and put in a holding cell without a phone in it. The next morning, he was taken down to the bond court where, because of a prior felony conviction, he was given a $50,000 "D" bond. From bond court, he was taken to the jail for intake and processing and, although there is a bank of payphones in one of the holding cells in the jail intake area, Thomas was put in a holding cell with no phones and did not see a telephone until that night when he was taken to the medium security tier the jail assigned him to. Unfortunately, despite the three pay phones on the wall, Thomas still was not able to make a phone call:

> Author: So, you go through this long process and then you get upstairs. At that point were you able to make a phone call?
>
> The phones is broken. The phones is broken. So, that's another thing. You get up there, you know for sure that the phones won't work and the phones didn't work when I was there. We was complaining about making a phone call and the phone is broke. [The COs] say, "I guess somebody must of broke them that was in there before," so they don't make no effort to fix them. So somebody must, whoever got angry and broke the phones we all gotta suffer.

A week later, Thomas was transferred to a different tier and he finally got access to a working telephone. He immediately called his mother and asked her to call his boss, but it was too late.

> I told [my mom] I had been locked up and she said that, she asked me what was it for. She wanted to ask me, what should I do. I said, well, I told her to call the job. But when I did talk to her again she said the job had terminated me.
>
> Author: OK. For not showing up?
>
> For not showing up and not calling in for seven days or more. It was three days, you know, by the time I called my mom it was like about over ten days or so and when she did finally call and I talked to her it took me another week or so to talk to her again, you know. She told me I had been terminated.

Thomas eventually pleaded guilty to the forgery charge and was sentenced to time served plus two years on probation and released. Of course, it is conceivable that he would have lost his job as a consequence of this conviction even if he had never been detained, although it is impossible to know, since he was fired long before he took a guilty plea. When I interviewed him two and a half years after his detention, he still had not found another job. "It's my record," he explained, noting that, despite his previous luck finding a job with a felony record, it was not easy to do so.

Unlike Thomas, Sam, who I introduced in Chapter 3, did get in touch with his employer during his detention. A White man in his mid-30s who was arrested when the police mistook his laundry detergent for cocaine, Sam was working as a house painter at the time of his arrest. Having been part of the same crew for several years, he felt like he had a good enough relationship with his boss to call him from the jail and explain the situation.

> Author: Did you contact the painting company from jail?
> I did.
> Author: What did you tell them?
> I told [my boss] what happened. He said, "I need to replace you because we need to get things done. I can't sit and wait for you, I'm sorry. You're a good worker but there's nothing I can do. You know what I have to do." I said "yes, I understand."

Six weeks later, toxicology lab results came back confirming Sam's innocence. The judge dismissed the charges against Sam and he was released. Unfortunately, the painting company where he had been working had already replaced him.

> [My boss] said "if there's a spot available when you get out, I'll let you know."
> Author: Did you contact them when you got out?
> Yeah, no spot available so I lost the job.

Reflecting on the experience a couple of years later, the job loss continued to gnaw at Sam, who explicitly associates his job loss with an unjust criminal justice system that did not work for him.

> Author: How did that make you feel that you had been locked up for 40 days on [dropped] charges?
> Very, you know, upset, angry, I felt like the system didn't work for me. I understood if I did something wrong. Or if there was even suspicion. I was pulled over on a traffic stop and I had a box of laundry supplies… But the whole experience I thought, I was so elated to get out but I just felt like my wings were clipped. I lost my job and they messed me up. I felt I was unjustly treated.

Of course, using the Court's reasoning in the *US v. Salerno* and *Bell v. Wolfish* decisions, Sam's case could be considered a success: an innocent man was cleared of wrongdoing, the charges against him were dismissed, and he was released. Despite the fact that Sam never went to trial, his case could nonetheless be seen as evidence that the presumption of innocence worked. From Sam's perspective—and, I argue, that of any reasonable observer—however, not only did his detention make clear that he was not presumed innocent, but it also subjected him to a series of collateral punishments that had repercussions long past his release. Beyond having been punished by being detained, Sam's experience is clear evidence of the direct economic detriment of pretrial detention independent of case outcome. Unlike Thomas, who may have lost his job when he was convicted even if he had not been detained pretrial, Sam's employer made clear that it was Sam's absence that led to his termination, even though he was never convicted of the charge for which he was detained.

"It Puts You in the Hole, You Know"

While loss of employment is undoubtedly one of the most noteworthy financial implications of pretrial detention, it is by no means the only one. Even people who do not lose their jobs while detained suffer financially as a result of their time in jail due to lost wages and other costs associated with detention. Beyond this, there are a variety of other costs that people incur, ranging from fees for vehicles impounded during arrest to child care costs for parents to transportation costs for family members traveling to and from the jail. As I discuss below, these costs, like job loss, do not differentiate between defendants who are convicted and those who are not.

A small number of detainees manage to hold onto their jobs but still experience financial hardship because of lost wages and missed bill payments. Rick, a White man in his 50s, owned his own plumbing business when he was arrested outside a city-run warming center on a cold day in winter.

> It's a very well-known drug spot. I've never been convicted of doing any drugs, I don't do any drugs. I was in a place called Rothschild's Liquor Store and I came out and I don't know if they were detectives or just plain clothes police officers. And I walked out with my product, walking back to the Chicago Department of Human Services, which is a warming shelter. And, they pulled me over and brought me to the car and took everything out of my pockets and told me, first I asked why, I asked why I was being detained and they said that because normally White people don't come to this neighborhood. And

I said "well, if you have to go to Human Services you have to be in this neighborhood." And they went through my wallet and pulled everything out and threw everything on the ground and basically that was it for about five minutes. And then they ran my name through the computer and saw that I was arrested before and then they took me down to the station.

When he arrived at the police station, Rick found out that he was being charged with possession of a controlled substance, a charge he denies. Like other arrested individuals, Rick was transported to the courthouse where he was placed in a holding cell for a few hours before his bond court appearance. When he finally went before the judge, Rick was dismayed to find out that his bond was being set at $5,000 "C"—cash only.

> And they set me at $5,000, cash only, no bond, no ten percent, five thousand cash only. And that was the amazing thing I'm trying to figure out.

Rick's contention that he did not have drugs on him appears to be validated by the fact that three and a half weeks later his charges were dropped. Having had no more court appearances, no information about the case, and no interactions with the public defender's office, Rick was released.

> Author: So how long after your bond court was your next court hearing?
> I didn't have another court hearing.
> Author: You never had another court hearing?
> Nope.
> Author: OK, so how did you find out you were being released?
> They came up there. I was sleeping and it was like 5:30 in the morning and the next thing I know – swisssssshhhhh – the door came open and [the COs] pulled me out... They took me right down to property and I'm going okay, "what's going on here?" And they said that "the charges against you have been dismissed." After three and a half weeks it's automatically it's like this, you know. And they, yeah. They dress you out and that was basically it.

Although owning his own business protected him from being terminated during the three and a half weeks that he was detained, it did not insulate Rick from lost income during that time, nor from other expenses related to his detention. In addition to losing income and clients, Rick also had to deal with extra costs from missing bill payments while in jail.

> I lost a couple of clients because, you know, people were calling back and stuff like that to have me come and there's no answer. And so they had to get somebody else. So I dropped a little bit of, you know, business and stuff like that. But, nothing really that bad with my business that I couldn't make up.
>
> Author: OK. So [the financial issues were] just mostly the not working for three and a half weeks?
>
> Yeah, it puts you in the hole, you know. 'Cause when you have bills to pay and child support and stuff like that, you know. And nobody wants to hear, you know, and everybody assumes, well, "where've you been for the last month?" "Oh, I've been in Cook County Jail."

As Rick observed, "it doesn't make a difference" to clients who found out that he was in jail that he was neither actually nor legally guilty of the charges for which he was detained—being in jail did not reflect positively on him and the assumption was always that he would not have been there if he had not done anything wrong. It also made no difference to his landlord, his child support payments, or his other bills; being in jail may have eliminated his income but it did not eliminate expenses.

Tarik, a 24-year-old Black man, managed to keep his job as an airline baggage handler during his detention by getting coworkers to cover his shifts. Arrested for drug possession after being searched during a routine traffic stop, Tarik also managed to borrow enough money from his friends and family to bond out of jail after 30 days. Needing to make up for lost wages and repay those who were helping him with his bond, Tarik put in extra time at work to help cover costs. Despite this, he was not able to make enough money to recover his car, which had been impounded in the course of his arrest.

> Author: So what happened with [your car]? If you were locked up for a month?
>
> I had to leave it in [the pound]. It was either get my car out [for] $1,000 or get myself out [for] $1,000.
>
> Author: So you lost your car?
>
> Basically I lost my car. Now I'm back on the CTA [Chicago Transit Authority], public transportation. But hey, I'd rather be

on the CTA than in jail and a car ain't nothing but material. I can always buy me another car. It was my baby though, my first car. 1994 convertible. But hey you get that chance to have good times and you get that chance to lose it. You know, everything's not forever.

Notwithstanding his philosophical attitude regarding the loss of his car, this issue is one of many financial hardships that respondents experienced as a consequence of their pretrial detentions, and one about which few are as stoic as Tarik.

As discussed in Chapter 3, Nicole's car was also impounded when she was arrested and she had to pay $800 to get it back, despite the charges against her being dismissed. Roseanne, a White woman in her 60s who eventually plead guilty to a DUI charge, never got her car back.

No, I never got my car back. I didn't have enough money to get it.
   Author: You never got your car back?
   No.
   Author: And it's still there?
   No. It's squashed. They sent me a letter that said since I didn't claim it they were going to do that, you know. And I knew with a DUI I might not be able to drive anyway. But I thought that you know, maybe because it's so expensive too. It's $125—$200 then $125 for the first four days, each day. And then $25 after that per day. And they only hold it for 20 days.

Like Tarik, Roseanne was able to borrow enough money to get out on bail after only a few weeks in pretrial detention but by the time she was out the cost of getting her car back was exorbitant. She decided that the money would be better spent hiring a defense attorney and left her car at the pound. When I asked Roseanne if she could estimate the monetary cost of losing her car, she just shook her head and sighed.

Although the largest, cars are by no means the only possessions people lose as a result of their detentions. Respondents who live alone often lose their apartments when they cannot pay rent during their detentions; in many cases, losing an apartment also means losing all of the possessions inside it.

Thomas, who pleaded guilty to forgery charges after several months in custody, is an example of this. At the time of his arrest,

Thomas was living alone and, unable to pay rent while detained, he eventually lost his apartment. Notwithstanding losing his place to live, Thomas was less concerned about the apartment itself than about all of the possessions that were now unattended. His concerns were well founded and by the time his sister went to check on his apartment, everything was gone.

> I had an apartment and no one was left in the apartment. I had left some, nobody was there to see about my apartment. And in the process a lot of things was stolen out of my apartment 'cause I wasn't there. So, after about, I think about three months my sister finally got to my apartment and she said everything was missing. So somebody knew that I was gone.
>
> Author: What about your apartment? What happened to that?
>
> I lost the apartment. I lost all the furniture and the TV, DVD set. I had a nice entertainment system and I lost all that. And, the guy that I rent it from I tried to get another apartment in his complex and he said no. He said I just left and I destroyed the apartment 'cause whoever went in there they just tore the apartment apart, taking things up.

Kevin, a Black man in his 40s, who was battling a drug addiction when he was arrested for possession of a controlled substance, was living in a recovery house at the time of his arrest. He had already lost his job and most of his possessions as a consequence of his drug addiction and what little he had was at the recovery house where he was staying. After three and a half months in jail, Kevin pleaded guilty and was released on probation. He returned to the same recovery house to continue his treatment but his possessions were long gone.

> The main thing was all my clothes were there and I was concerned about I would lose my clothes. I called and let them know I was in jail, but like, that's a recovery house and people come and go in there you know.
>
> Author: Were you able to get in touch with anybody there?
>
> I didn't get in touch, well, when I got arrested I did because they tried to put me on house arrest but they like, somebody was there on house arrest and they can't have two house arrest people in the same house so I had to stay in jail.
>
> Author: And what ended up happening to your stuff?
>
> I lost it.

Author: They threw it out?

No, they said they ain't know nothing about it. You know, like, it's not too structured. The organization [the recovery house], it's like, it's not too structured, like I said. Like, I let one of the guys know that, he knew my stuff was there and he was going to put it in the basement and then they threw it out. Which I doubt. They probably just gave it away or—I was upset about it.

In many ways, Kevin's experience highlights much of the illogic of the pretrial detention system. He admits that he was guilty of the crime with which he was charged and he had a prior conviction for felony possession of a controlled substance. Despite this, the court recognized that he did not pose a high risk to public safety and wanted to place him on house arrest pending adjudication; because court rules prohibit two people from being on house arrest in any single residence, however, Kevin had to stay in jail instead. When he agreed to plead guilty three and a half months later, he was given a standard sentence of probation with the condition that he enter a drug treatment program and, upon release, he returned to the exact same substance abuse treatment center that he had been living in prior to his arrest and detention. The only difference was that now he had one more felony conviction and fewer personal possessions.

In contrast to the concrete, measurable costs of missing work, losing a job, or having a car impounded, the economic costs of lost time and missed opportunities are not so easily quantifiable. Several respondents who were unemployed and looking for work when they were arrested missed job interviews and possibly jobs as well. In addition, a number of respondents were in school at the time of their arrests and most were unable to make up the time and schoolwork that they missed while locked up.

Marlon, who we met in the last chapter, lost out on both a promising job opportunity and a semester of school. As discussed in Chapter 3, Marlon was arrested on a Sunday, after being falsely accused of assault by a neighbor who was mad about not being invited to a neighborhood barbeque. At 22 years old, Marlon was a fulltime student who was also working to help support his young son. Shortly before his arrest, he had lost his job at a downtown retail chain and had been busy looking for something else. The week before he was arrested, Marlon had had an interview that went well at another retail outlet and he had been asked to come back for a second interview and to bring his ID and social security card. Unfortunately for him, that interview was scheduled for the day after he was arrested, and he never made it.

> Author: You mentioned you had this job interview the next day?
> Yes, I was worried about that because I just recently lost my job in April and I was working downtown at [a department store] and I lost my job and I was going through it because you know, I have a son to take care of and I needed money and I just finally got this, this job offer basically. The lady basically told me "oh, okay, come in for the interview but when you come make sure you bring your ID and your social security card." So I was thinking okay, well, you know, I'm gonna get this job and now I'm going to jail the day before.

Although Marlon tried to get a family member to contact the store, it did not work out, and he lost the job opportunity.

> I tried to have my family, my dad call when I got locked up. I told him, you know, make sure you call them and let them know that I'm having a family emergency and I can't come. But, when I got out I found out that he couldn't find the number, he didn't know the number to them.
> Author: So they just think you didn't show up?
> Right.

Compounding the frustration for Marlon, when he was released from jail three weeks after his arrest, he quickly discovered that he had missed too much schoolwork to complete the semester and would have to restart the classes the next term.

> Author: You said you were in school. So what happened with your school for those three weeks?
> Actually, I lost three weeks of school. So, I have to do that whole semester over, 'cause I was too far behind. So, I gotta get back, get back on that, on top of that, next, next month.
> Author: It feels like a lot?
> Yeah…

Amid three and a half weeks in jail, a missed job opportunity, and a lost semester of school, the one break that Marlon caught was that his godmother worked in the administration at the culinary institute he attended and she was able to arrange for the tuition he had already paid to be applied to the following semester.

"It's My Fault Because She Don't Have Enough Money for the Rent."

For Sarah, a stay-at-home mom with seven children between the ages of two and 18, the biggest opportunity loss was to her 18-year-old daughter, who missed school to watch Sarah's younger children during the 45 days she was detained. Like Kevin, whose experience I discussed earlier in this chapter, Sarah was battling a drug addiction and admits that she was guilty of possession of a controlled substance. Also like Kevin, Sarah finally pleaded guilty to possession of a controlled substance and was released after receiving the standard sentence of two years on probation. Despite being released upon admitting guilt, some of the consequences of her detention were irreversible, including some of the consequences for her family.

> Certain days [my oldest daughter] had to miss out of school to take care of my younger kids, the ones that wasn't in school. And, she had to miss days out of school and when she did go to school my cousin would come over and watch the kids until she got out of school… I really don't know how much school she missed but it's like, after I did come home it was like she wasn't really interested in going to school no more. Because she used to be an honor student and then failed down [while I was in jail], you know. So, then she just stopped going to school and I said, "no you need to go back to school. You're a senior and you're getting ready to graduate." You know. So now she's currently pregnant, two months pregnant, and she's not in school.
>
> Author: And you feel like that's partially because when she missed school she felt like there wasn't really a point of going back?
>
> Yeah, because I guess she figured she didn't want to be 19 or 20 and graduate. I said it doesn't matter as long as you graduate.

Sarah is by no means the only respondent whose family suffered either lost opportunities or more direct financial consequences as a result of the respondent's detention. For many people, even small costs have a big effect. Charles, who was a fulltime student when he was arrested, was living with his girlfriend who worked fulltime, just barely earning enough to cover the rent. Although Charles had not been contributing substantially to household costs, his detention created new costs, including transportation to and from the jail, collect calls, and commissary, that they could not afford.

It's a lot of money problems because my girl get paid like $700–800 a month, she pays $500 in rent. But somehow because of the one day she got a bye because she needed to come to court and my visiting days.

Author: How did she get to come see you?

The bus card, them bus cards are expensive. $5.75 for one day. Then $22 for seven days. But she doing this every week, every week she's spending $25. Then she's spending more money if she lose her bus card. This girl lose bus cards like it ain't nothing, they don't cost $22. She go buy another bus card. Then it got to the point it was so bad with money was so tight that she paid $200 on the rent. The rent is $500 and she paid $200 on the rent. She couldn't come up with the rest. She had to go to the [community center] and get a box of food, you know.

Author: This was all while you were locked up?

Yeah... It's my fault why she gotta keep running back and forth. It's my fault because she don't have enough money for the rent. I'm talking to her on the phone from County [jail] and she like, 'I'm $300 short on money.' I can't do anything about that, I'm in here. It's my fault for all of that.

Notes

1 From Foote (1965a).
2 https://niccc.csgjusticecenter.org/
3 See, in particular, Kohler-Hausmann's (2018) and Natapoff's (2018) respective work on misdemeanors, which offer distinct but mutually reinforcing views on the high costs of misdemeanor arrests and other "subfelony" justice system contact; and the growing body of work on criminal justice financial obligations (LFOs), including Shannon et al. (2020); Beckett et al. (2008); and Martin et al. (2018), to name a few.

5 "The Pains Of Imprisonment"[1]

Brian thought he was already at the low point in his life before his arrest and subsequent 86 days in jail. He had been laid off from his job as a lab technician several months before and, after separating from his wife of almost 20 years, was living at his mother's house. To cope with the stress of unemployment and likely divorce, a friend had recently introduced him to heroin. Brian knew that his heroin use was a problem, but the thought of spending time in jail had never occurred to him: other than one arrest more than 15 years before—for which the charges were quickly dismissed—he had always been a model citizen, never getting in trouble, always working hard, and trying to set a good example for his kids.

On March 17, 2009, that all changed. Brian was standing outside a convenience store smoking a cigarette when he was approached by a Chicago Police Department officer. Acting on a tip that a Black man wearing a black jacket and blue pants was selling heroin, the officer approach Brian—a Black man wearing a brown shirt and gray pants—and searched him. The search quickly turned up two bags of heroin, not enough for a distribution arrest, but certainly enough to arrest Brian for possession of a controlled substance.

Brian's first concern was about his family, especially as the hours passed by and he still was not able to call them.

> [T]hey arrested me on the spot, then I had to stay in this hold over thing because I got arrested about 12 that day and one of they procedure is, you have all of these district stations around Chicago and, you don't get a bond, or you don't have a bond, they just sit you in there. If you want to bond out, you have no bond. One of the things that is a problem is, they have no record you're in there or where you at. So, I couldn't even let my people know where I was at until after I went to court the next day.

Early the next morning Brian was picked up from the district station holding cell and brought to the courthouse for bond court. Despite having only one prior arrest and no prior convictions, his bail was set at $75,000 "D" bond, with a $7,500 deposit required for release. Brian's charge, although a felony, was nonviolent, and Brian, with two bags of heroin, was unlikely to pose a risk to public safety, but the fact that he was unemployed and living with his mother likely indicated instability to the prosecutor and the judge. Regardless of the reason for the high bail, Brian knew that there was no way he could come up with $7,500. The stress began to wear on his already fragile mental health immediately.

> Author: What went through your head [when you heard your bond]?
> Actually, I got into a little altercation with a guy [in the holding cell] because I was pissed off. Because, first of all, I told you how crowded it was back there—the next thing he kept on stepping on my feet. Intentionally. And after all that [the bond hearing], I kind of blew up back there.

After he was taken from court and booked into the jail, Brian's experience largely mirrored those described in prior chapters. Like others detained for the first time, Brian was taken aback at the callousness of the correctional officers and the generally dehumanizing experience of being in jail.

> You know, to me personally, they shouldn't put people in, I call it, an unhumane situation, because that's exactly what it is. That's what they do in there. They put you in unhumane circumstances... The thing that kind of upset me about the whole thing, even though you're a mannerable person, don't give them no trouble, they treated everybody the same, like they were hardened criminals.

Also like others detained for the first time, Brian assumed that his case would be processed fairly quickly and he would be out in a matter of days. As the time progressed, his health and mental health continued to decline. Between the discomfort of sleeping on a bunk-bed in a small cell with three strangers and the stress and loneliness of the situation, Brian could not sleep. He had a hard time eating too and began losing weight. As he recalled during our interview, "I lost 22 pounds while I was in there. It was 84 days and I lost 22 pounds...

I couldn't eat." More than anything, Brian missed his family and felt increasingly isolated and disconnected from the outside world.

> Yeah, my wife, well, estranged wife, she came and visited me. My mother, she came to visit me every visiting day... That's the only thing you look forward to is a visit or at least some mail from somebody. That gives you a connection with the outside world because once you in there you don't see no semblances of real life. You just, everything is weird and whatever. My mother came and saw me every visiting day, my wife and my sons they came to visit me too. So that was cool. I looked forward to that. When them days come, I was perky. The rest of that stuff I was depressed, really.

Realizing that he was depressed, Brian inquired about mental health services, something that he had never sought out before.

> The rest of the time I was depressed, really. I even tried to see some people in there. I never did see them.
>   Author: Like a counselor or something?
>   Yeah.
>   Author: Because you were depressed?
>   Yeah, try to deal with some depression.

Like other people held in pretrial detention, Brian was also becoming increasingly disillusioned with the criminal legal process. Consistent with the experiences described in Chapters 2 and 3, Brian's encounters with criminal justice practitioners—including judges, defense counsel, and correctional officers—and the criminal justice process—including rapid and incomprehensible court hearings, repeated continuances, and a seemingly endless detention—were making it clear that he was presumed guilty by all and that, ultimately, a guilty plea was his only way out of custody.

> I was at the mercy of the public defender. I didn't have options. Nobody gave me the impression that they was going to fight for me because it's the culture in there: if you're in there you're guilty. You guilty until you proven guilty. You're guilty because, "if you was innocent you wouldn't be here." That's what [the COs] always say. "If you was innocent you wouldn't be here."

After 84 days in jail, Brian pleaded guilty and was released onto probation. By this time, it was clear to him that dominant notions about the criminal legal system were a farce.

> I'm not saying that what I did was alright. I'm just saying, you're still supposed to get due process. Due process is out the door. Nobody's looking at that. They just saying "they criminals anyway." Everybody is not a bad person. They just made an error in judgment.

Pretrial Detention and Mental Health

Gresham Sykes first detailed "the pains of imprisonment" in his seminal work, *The Society of Captives* (1958/2007), arguing that, contrary to the widespread belief that prisons are a more humane alternative to pervasive use of corporal punishment in the past, the psychological harms of incarceration "can be just as painful as the physical maltreatment which they have replaced" (p. 64). Since that time, a sizeable body of scholarship has documented the negative effects of incarceration on the mental health of people in prison, making clear the profound harm of carceral confinement to people's mental well-being (Adams 1992; Haney 2002, 2006; Porporino 1992; Poporino and Zamble 1984; Zamble 1992). Although most research on pretrial detention and mental health focuses primarily on documenting the prevalence of mental health disorders and co-occurring mental health and substance use disorders among individuals held in pretrial detention, and in jails more generally, without paying much attention to the effect of pretrial detention on the mental health of people who are detained, several of the key findings from the research on imprisonment and mental health have particular relevance for thinking about pretrial detention's effects on people's mental health.

Two well-established findings on incarceration and mental health are particularly applicable: first, research on incarceration and mental health has consistently shown that "the initial stage of confinement is the greatest risk period for emotional disorder, suicide, self-injury, and violent and disruptive behavior" (Adams 1992: 328–329). Unsurprisingly, being incarcerated is traumatic, and no more so at any point than following the initial transition from freedom to confinement (Haney 2006; Walker et al. 2014; Zamble 1992).[2]

Second, research has shown that increased uncertainty has a negative effect on the mental health of people who are incarcerated.

Indeterminate sentencing, wherein sentence length is not predetermined, but is decided by a parole board with significant discretion, has been identified as one of the primary causes of stress and anxiety for people who are incarcerated (Goodstein 1980; Mason 1990). Reviewing research on the psychological toll of indeterminate sentencing, Mason (1990) concluded that the adverse psychological effects are so clear as to indicate that indeterminate sentencing actually constitutes cruel and unusual punishment.[3]

Not surprisingly, one of the few studies examining the effect of pretrial detention on the mental health of people who are detained found that, in contrast to people who are in prison, people who are detained pretrial show increasing anxiety over time. Oleski (1977), whose study on anxiety among pretrial detainees is one of the few to show the anxiety levels increasing over the course of confinement rather than decreasing, argued that this was at least partially due to elevated anxiety related to the uncertainty of pretrial detention. Unlike people held in prison who are generally able to settle into and acclimate to institutional life after a stressful initial adjustment, individuals detained pretrial are in a perpetual state of uncertainty that precludes adjustment. Knowing neither how long their current detention will last nor what the outcome of their adjudication will be, people detained pretrial thus experience increased anxiety over the course of their detention.

"I was Missing My Kids. My Little Sister..."

No respondent summed up the psychological impact of pretrial detention better than David, a Black man in his 50s who has been detained several times for drug possession and other crimes related to his substance use disorder:

> The County jail is, it's a place that if you're not strong, it will break you. It will break you down because you might be missing your family and the people in there, they don't care. They don't care about what you going through, what you facing, you be demoralized, you barely get a haircut, you barely get a change of clothes. You might have to wear the same clothes for months. You just gotta keep washing them out in the toilet or wherever. And if you're not a strong person they'll break you down. When I was there a couple of guys committed suicide—attempted—somebody was there to in the nick of time to be coming through and looking and saved they life. So if you're not strong they will break you down 'til you be going on the psycho ward.

When I asked David to elaborate on the reasons why being detained can "break you down," his explanation largely mapped to the findings in the scholarship referenced above, pointing to both the general conditions of confinement and to the specific uncertainty experienced by those still awaiting the resolution of the criminal legal process.

> The, it's just, it can be a lot of things like me not having nobody to call. So a person could be in there to have somebody to call, they're not accepting their phone calls. So that got them down. The [correctional officers] start hollering, tell you—because something they did, that can break you down. Then you not getting the proper medical attention you need, that can break you down. Or if anybody is sending you money, your money gets lost. Or they not giving you the proper amount of commissary, that can break you down. It's the whole gloominess of the County [jail] can break you, all that built up in one can break a person down. They don't know how much time they face, it's probably they first time ever. The people in there [say] "oh, you gonna go down, you gonna get this much time, do this, do that", or they say "you going home," but when you go to the judge the judge say "you ain't going home." So they got your hopes up and you go to the judge and the judge say, "no, you'll do the whole thing." When you get back in that cell there's no one except a roommate who don't want to hear it.

As scholars have long noted, isolation from family and friends and the corresponding loneliness are among the most emotionally taxing aspects of incarceration. The people I interviewed would certainly agree, and feelings of isolation and loneliness were one of the most commonly identified causes of depression. Tarik, the respondent from Chapter 4 who chose to pay for his bail rather than retrieve his impounded car, explains the importance of being in contact with family and friends while in custody.

> Every day I stayed on the phone trying to call somebody to make sure if anything is going on, what's looking up.
>   Author: You would call people to check on your case or did you feel like you needed to talk to someone outside so that you felt okay?
>   Both. To talk about my case, to see what types of advantages and disadvantages I had. Basically, just to keep myself sane. Being in jail is depressing.

Charles also noted the importance of being in touch with people to his mental health while detained. He, like many respondents, expressed his frustration with the phones in the jail, which cannot receive calls and are set up in such a way as to preclude many outgoing calls, exacerbating the psychological toll of pretrial detention by increasing detainees' isolation:

> The pay phones are messed up too. I think that's something that they should deal with because you get through to nobody on those phones.
> Author: Did you try to use the phone?
> Yeah, I tried a lot of times. You can't even get to nobody on those phones. The only way I got through on that phone was when I saw my girlfriend in court—wait, when I saw my girlfriend when she came to visit me. I told her to take the block off the phone. There could be a block on there that you don't even know there's a block on there. They can block that phone call but they don't block no other collect calls…
> Author: Who else did you try to call?
> I tried to call my brother, my momma, my sister, my auntie, all the numbers is restricted. I know all the numbers don't have blocks on the phones. All the numbers are restricted. They shouldn't do that. People need to call. That's what keep people head up instead of going crazy.

Similarly, Marlon, the young man who was detained for three weeks before his neighbor admitted that her accusation of battery was false, also noted that the general strain of being detained was exacerbated by his feelings of isolation. "Emotionally I was just, I just felt lonely, like nobody cared about me. Um, personally, um, I don't know, I just felt all by myself. Nobody, you know, nobody was there to help me."

While the most acute psychological toll of detention fades for most people following their release from custody, a number of people did talk about struggling with feelings of depression, anger, and anxiety long after they were released. Brian, whose story began this chapter, broke down in tears at several points during our conversation, which took place six months following his release.

> I made a mistake okay and I take responsibility for that. But at the same time, my mother don't say it, but she's kind of disappointed. My son don't say it, but he's disappointed too because,

especially my older son, he always looked up to me and this is something that they never went through. I have five children, all of them grown and stuff, not one of them ever been arrested or went to jail for a parking ticket. I kind of like raised the bar for them... That part is kind of hard for me right now. I go to a lot of, I see a lot of counselors right now because this stuff is wearing on me, Mikaela.

Procedural Justice

Brian was somewhat unique in highlighting and discussing at length his ongoing mental health struggles related to his detention and concomitant circumstances. Instead, when most people reflected on or alluded to the non-material implications of their detentions, they spoke primarily about feelings of anger and disillusionment, of having been mistreated and having been wronged.

In this way, people's experiences largely typify the procedural justice literature, which argues that people's experiences with the criminal justice *process* inform their attitudes toward the criminal justice system more than any particular criminal justice *outcomes* (Rosenfeld and Fornango 2014; Sunshine and Tyler 2003; Tyler 2003).[4] Research on procedural justice in the criminal justice context has focused primarily on policing and, particularly in the years since Michael Brown's murder and the emergence of the Black Lives Matter movement, sought to identify ways to improve the relationships between law enforcement agencies and Black communities. Toward this end, this work has identified four central features of people's interactions with law enforcement have the greatest effect on their belief in the legitimacy of law enforcement: "whether they were treated with dignity and respect, whether they were given voice, whether the decision-maker was neutral and transparent, and whether the decision-maker conveyed trustworthy motives" (Quattlebaum et al. 2018: 6; see also Bradford 2014; Meares 2009; President's Task Force on 21st Century Policing 2015; Stanford SPARQ 2018; Tyler 2017).

In the wake of George Floyd's murder and the growing movement to defund or, at minimum, fundamentally remake policing, it may seem naïve to argue that more procedurally just policing will increase trust toward and legitimacy of law enforcement among African Americans or more broadly. Nonetheless, the framework that procedural justice provides for reckoning with the implications of unjust criminal justice processes can help elucidate the ways in which the injustices of pretrial detention have larger consequences for people's belief in the legitimacy of the criminal justice system.

"After I Went Through All that, I Hated Police for a Minute, I Just Hated them."

Of course, the extent to which people were disillusioned by their experiences with pretrial detention was directly related to their perspectives about and expectations of the criminal justice system prior to being detained. Thus, for most of the White people I interviewed and for African Americans from middle class backgrounds the shock and disillusionment was acute. By contrast, for African American respondents from poor neighborhoods or who had more exposure to the criminal justice system, their personal experiences with pretrial detention and the criminal legal system more generally served to validate what they already knew regarding the fairness and legitimacy of the criminal justice system.

Rick, the White man from Chapter 4 whose plumbing business suffered when he was detained on a possession of a controlled substance charge that was subsequently declined for prosecution by the states attorney's office, noted that the experience had completely altered his beliefs about the justice system. In contrast to his previous belief that "If you didn't do anything wrong… everything will be okay," his attitude toward and perception of the criminal justice system has now changed; "Now, the law to me is nothing now, nothing but a business. I mean, it's a complete and utter sham to me."

Nicole and Sam, the respondents I spoke with whose respective drug possession charges were dismissed when lab results showed that neither had been in possession of a controlled substance, expressed a similar disillusionment. As noted in Chapter 3, Sam, a White man in his 30s, expressed shock and anger with his realization that "the [justice] system didn't work for me."

Nicole, a Black woman in her 50s with no prior experience with the criminal justice system, spoke of both the anger that she felt in the immediate aftermath of her arrest and detention, and the persistent fear that she still experienced almost a year later. In describing her hatred for police following her experience, she also evidenced her mistrust and cynicism.

> Actually, to tell you the truth after I went through all that, I hated police for a minute, I just hated them. I wasn't no lawbreaker. The fact that they can get what they want and do

what they want. It was just not, I'm thinking about all the other folks in there. Most of them aren't real criminals. The REAL criminals y'all ain't caught. You wasting my time.

As she continued, her fear also became clear.

I actually just got my driving license back. That's because I was just done. I didn't know about anything, I just went down and started the process so I can get it back. He said "you're fine, everything's paid." That's what I did at the court when I came back. When I tell you, now I'm scared to drive.

Consistent with other findings regarding the effect of being detained, neither people's actual guilt or innocence, nor their eventual case outcomes meaningfully differentiated how they assessed the fairness of pretrial detention and the associated criminal justice system processes. While Rick, Sam, and Nicole all had their charges dismissed—an ostensibly fair outcome, given their actual innocence—Ron acknowledged his guilt and pleaded guilty, but still reported a comparable sense of disillusionment in the aftermath of his experience.

A White man in his 40s, Ron was arrested at a pharmacy when he tried to fill a prescription for weight loss drugs that he had illegally obtained online. When I spoke with him, he acknowledged that the prescription may have been illegal, but argued that there was no way for him to know that. Although he eventually pleaded guilty, he continued to feel like he was mistreated by a system that should have pursued the online organization that provided him with the prescription rather than prosecuting him for an accidental and minor crime.

I'm sorry to be so emphatic about it. I'm emotional about it because I just think I'm wronged. But, you know, what can I do, you know.

Author: So I guess that's part of what I want to know. We talked about specific [consequences of this experience] but I guess more generally, how do you see this whole experience as having affected you, your life, and the people close to you?

It has created even greater cynicism with our society... So, I, so it has affected my life. It has affected my life and it has affected, probably affected me for the rest of my life. Every time you're arrested it affects you for the rest of your life.

Author: Just in terms of your attitude?

Attitude towards society.

For Duane and Terrance, both Black men who lived in low income South Side neighborhoods and had been arrested a couple of times before, being detained served to validate what they already knew about the criminal justice system. Duane spent six months in custody in lieu of $2,500 (on a $25,000 "D" bond) following an arrest for a theft. Although he was quick to acknowledge that he was "a little wild," his experience while detained did nothing to increase his trust in the system. In particular, the fact that the prosecutor kept requesting continuances and the judge kept granting them, despite both knowing that he was sitting in jail in the meantime, made it clear that there was nothing fair about the process. The fact that the prosecutor dropped the charges against Duane after he spent six months in custody only served to reinforce Duane's mistrust for the criminal justice process, despite the ostensibly just final outcome.

> They kept offering me three years for a theft and then I said no I ain't taking that because I know I wasn't the one so they finally, after six months, they wound up dropping it... and the killer part about it was, I think they knew this was the way it was going to end out. That's the reason every time I would come to court, [the prosecutor] would have some excuse like, "the state is not ready yet." They can't get your witnesses together. First, they had witnesses and then they didn't have witnesses. Then there was another issue. Then that issue would disappear also, so they knew that they were going to have to dismiss the whole case.

For Terrance, a Black man who pleaded guilty to a trespassing charge that he denied having committed, the fact that the courts appeared to lend more credence to the police's description of events than to his without doing any research into the facts of the case showed that the whole criminal justice system was stacked against him. Terrance expressed doubt in either the fairness or the impartiality of the criminal legal system.

> You know, I think overall people [who work in the criminal justice system] are not concerned with facts when they are the people that are able to determine what is right and what is wrong. No one is really ready to dig in enough to find out the real facts of people's cases or what really actually happened. They are more always leaning on the side of the [police] than the person that is allegedly a perpetrator of a crime or whatever happens... It's all corrupt. It's all burned up to me.

"I Served this Country for Nothing."

A number of the individuals I spoke with were military veterans and, for these respondents, the sense of injustice and disillusionment was particularly acute. Reggie and Calvin, the respondents whose stories start Chapters 2 and 3 respectively, especially underscored their struggles to reconcile their service to their country with the mistreatment they experienced upon their return. Reggie, who served in a special operations unit in the Army, explained the resentment that he is still grappling to come to terms with:

> It is real ironic, you know. I guess that's something that I constantly deal with on an everyday basis. That, here it is. I was over in Lebanon, put my life on the line for the country while I was over in Lebanon. I was part of the crew that went over and got Noriega from Panama and I was part of one of the training crews from Somalia. So, then to come home to the States and come back home to the United States and to be treated, to be treated like less than a man because that's the way you actually get treated when you in jail. You actually get treated like you less than a human being, really. That's not a good feeling at all. It makes you have some resentment. It makes you sit up and think, I served this country for nothing.

Calvin's comments largely echo Reggie's:

> [I was in the army for] four years. Then, it's like it doesn't matter. They don't care what you did. I don't know how they treat the police officers when they mess up and get arrested. But I know they don't send them to no, that County [jail] environment like we go through. But, you know what I'm saying, for somebody that served four years [in the Army], it's like to me I was just like a policeman, too, but I was a policeman for the country. And they put you in that cell for something you did or you *supposed* to have did, and then what you have to go through, it's really demeaning. The things you have to see when you in there. It's, it's like, it change your life. You can't put it no better, it would change your life 'cause you gonna come out a different person.

Although the contradiction between what Reggie and Calvin gave to their county and how they were treated in return makes their feelings of anger and resentment particularly poignant, their comments are also illustrative of the psychological evolution that many people experienced. Prior to their detentions, Reggie and Calvin expected to be treated with something more closely approximating fairness or justice. Their experiences, however, taught them otherwise, and in so doing, fundamentally altered their attitudes and beliefs about their country and, as Calvin put it, changed his life and turned him into a different person.

Notes

1 Sykes (1958/2007).
2 A series of books and articles by Zamble (1988, 1992), Zamble and Porporino (1990), and Zamble et al. (1984) describe a longitudinal investigation into the behavior, emotional state, and cognitions of people in prison after six months, 12 months, 18 months, and six and a half years in prison and found that their emotional wellbeing was significantly worse earliest in their prison stays across a variety of measures. Using the Beck Depression Inventory, the Hopelessness Scale, the Spielberger State Anxiety Inventory, and weekly reports of depression, anxiety, anger, guilt feelings, boredom, and loneliness, Zamble et al. (1984) found that respondents scored the highest on all measures at their six-month interviews and the lowest at their six and a half year interviews. MacKenzie and Goodstein (1985) compared incarcerated individuals with short-term and long-term sentences at various points in their prison terms and found the highest levels of anxiety, depression, psychosomatic illnesses, and fear among both groups earliest in peoples' sentences. Although people who were serving sentences of six years or more showed more anxiety at each point in time than people serving sentences of five years or less, the highest overall measures of all mental health variables were with prisoners at early points in their sentences.
3 Cole and Logan's (1977) survey of people held in state prisons found that 70 percent of respondents preferred fixed sentences to indefinite sentences, even if they might have to serve slightly more time. Messinger and Johnson (1978) noted that during the debate over a determinate sentencing bill in California, a lobby of current and formerly incarcerated people was the most prominent voice for determinate sentencing.
4 Of course, both police reform advocates and criminologists—as well as criminologists working on police reform—note the relationship between process and outcome. Campaign Zero and the Center for Policing Equity, for example, both advocate for police departments to implement policies changing the process of police/civilian interactions in order to reduce police violence. (See www.joincampaignzero.org and www.www.policingequity.org.) Similarly, Petersen and Omori (2020) show that, for Black defendants in particular, punitive processes also lead to punitive outcomes. The goal here is not to negate the relationship between process and outcome, but rather to highlight the ways in which the processes that characterize people's experiences with pretrial detention inform their attitudes toward the criminal justice system, regardless of their eventual criminal justice outcomes.

6   Looking Forward

At this very moment, somewhere in the range of 500,000 people are detained pretrial, sitting in county and federal jails all across the United States not because they have been convicted of crimes but because they cannot afford bail: incarcerated without conviction. Regardless of their actual guilt, the vast majority of these people will leave jail with criminal convictions, having chosen to plead guilty because their time in custody has led them to believe they have no other choice—every encounter they have with the criminal legal system and the practitioners therein assures them that the fastest—and often, it seems, the only—way out of custody is to plead guilty, effectively exchanging the presumption of innocence for their freedom.

The point here is not that all of the people whose experiences are described in this book, nor all individuals detained pretrial across the US, are factually innocent. To the contrary, over the course of this book, a number of respondents have acknowledged their own criminally illegal conduct; some of these individuals have gone on to prison, while others have been released post-conviction, given credit for time served in jail and/or placed under probation supervision.

Regardless of their actual guilt or innocence, the critical point is that the use of pretrial detention in the American criminal legal system fundamentally erodes any attempts to achieve justice therein. More people spend time in custody pretrial than post-conviction; people who have committed no crimes plead guilty to obtain release; people who have committed crimes forgo due process so as not to lengthen their confinements. In this context, what does justice mean? What value does innocence hold?

Nothing underscores the extent to which pretrial detention undermines the meaning of justice more than the experiences of those people who are never convicted for the crimes for which they are detained, those people who are both legally and factually innocent. Calvin, Aaron, Sam, Nicole, Marlon, Rick, and Duane spent weeks or months in jail only to have the charges against them dropped by prosecutors or dismissed by judges, or, in Aaron's case, to be acquitted at trial. Yet the legal affirmation of their actual innocence in no way alleviated the harm caused by being detained.

Indeed, neither the confinements nor the collateral consequences thereof for these never-convicted individuals differ substantively from the confinements and collateral consequences experienced by those whose cases end in conviction. Regardless of actual or legal guilt or innocence, people who are detained experience deep and lasting material and psychological harms. Jobs, homes, and possessions lost; opportunities and aspirations interrupted—these consequences do not differentiate between people who have engaged in criminal behavior and those who have not, nor between those who are ultimately convicted and those who are not. Rather, detention wreaks havoc on the lives and wellbeing of all defendants, as well as on their families and loved ones. Sam and Thomas both lost their jobs; Nicole and Tarik both lost their cars; Aaron and Charles both lamented the financial burden their detentions caused their already struggling families. The psychological harm that people experience while detained and the deep disillusionment that can persist for years thereafter is similar across defendants who are guilty or innocent, legally or factually. Defendants who plead guilty under the duress of detention and those who are never convicted have a shared experience of injustice that erodes their faith in the criminal legal system and, often, society more broadly. Given the findings presented here and in the larger body of research on pretrial detention, it would be hard to argue that their distrust is misplaced.

In addition to all of the harms detention wreaks on people's lives, the other critical collateral consequence of pretrial detention is its contribution to mass incarceration and the racial disparities therein. Being detained compels people to plead guilty and, when they do so, to accept more punitive plea deals than similarly situated defendants facing comparable criminal charges who are released pretrial, thus helping to drive conviction and incarceration rates, as well as sentence length. The fact that Black defendants are more likely to be detained pretrial than defendants from other racial/ethnic groups—a pattern demonstrated both in my sample of defendants from Cook County, IL, as well as in research from jurisdictions around the country, and which appears due in part to bias and in part to differential economic resources among defendants from different racial/ethnic groups—means that pretrial detention helps fuel the stark racial disparities in criminal justice outcomes.

Now What?

At this very moment, we have a unique opportunity to address these issues, to reform bail and pretrial detention policy across the United States, free hundreds of thousands of legally innocent people, and create a more just criminal legal system. Right now there is more attention to bail policy, more awareness of and outrage about the injustice of pretrial detention, than there has been at any point since the passage of the 1984 Federal Bail Reform Act. Both grassroots and high-profile advocacy and research organizations are increasingly focused on pretrial justice, and slowly policy changes are starting to occur. At the same time, a backlash has emerged to reverse the changes that have happened and prevent more substantial and widespread change from occurring. The achievement of meaningful and lasting changes to bail and pretrial justice is far from guaranteed and those of us who want to see a criminal legal system that truly presumes innocence and does not use detention to coerce guilty pleas have a long way to go. Below I provide a brief overview of the array of activism and policy changes that are afoot, as well as the backlash seeking to maintain the status quo.

In the years since #BlackLivesMatter, a number of grassroots racial justice groups have appropriately identified bail and pretrial detention as a critical nexus of racial injustice in a system rampant with racial disparities. Since 2017, the National Bail Out collective has had an annual #FreeBlackMamas campaign that calls attention to the detention of poor Black mothers by raising funds to bail out Black women who would otherwise be detained pretrial. Community bail funds, which raise money to pay the bail for individuals who would otherwise be detained pretrial, have become common across the US, and many—if not all—work not only to obtain people's release but also to advocate for bail and pretrial detention reform.

Simultaneously, a range of other high-profile organizations have turned their attention to issues related to bail and pretrial justice. The Vera Institute of Justice has undertaken significant research and advocacy efforts under the umbrella of its *Reducing the Use of Jails* Initiative, and a number of large philanthropic organizations have taken on this issue, foremost among them the MacArthur Foundation with its Safety and Justice Challenge, Arnold Ventures with its National Partnership for Pretrial Justice, and The Charles Koch Institute which focuses on pretrial justice as part of its efforts related to due process. Businesses have taken note as well. As mentioned in the first chapter of this book, Google and Facebook stopped accepting advertising from the bail bond industry in 2018, a decision that Google leaders credited to conversations with leaders from Koch Industries, the multinational corporation with subsidiaries across nearly a dozen industries, which has long supported criminal justice reform and has focused on bail and pretrial justice as of late.

Amid all of this attention, policymakers are taking note. In 2017, Senators Kamala Harris and Rand Paul introduced the Pretrial Integrity and Safety Act in the US Senate. While the bill died a quiet death after the senate majority leader declined to take it up for debate, the introduction of the first federal legislation seeking to increase pretrial release since the 1966 Bail Reform Act is still a noteworthy milestone. At least as noteworthy is the fact that Joe Biden's presidential campaign included the elimination of cash bail as part of its criminal justice platform. "End Cash Bail," his campaign website announced: "The cash bail system incarcerates people who are presumed innocent. And, it disproportionately harms low-income individuals. Biden will lead a national effort to end cash bail and reform our pretrial system by putting in place, instead, a system that is fair and does not inject further discrimination or bias into the process."[1]

Just as important are the policy changes taking place in states across the country. In 2019, New York State passed the Bail Elimination Act, spurred into action in large part by *TIME: The Kalief Browder Story* and associated advocacy efforts. In 2021, Illinois, where I conducted research for this book, passed the Pretrial Fairness Act, which will eliminate cash bail by 2023 and will strictly regulate the use of risk assessment algorithms and electronic monitoring. In addition to these changes, a number of states and counties across the country have taken legislative or executive action to reform bail and increase pretrial release, including the states of Alaska, Connecticut, New Mexico, New Jersey, and California,[2] as well as counties such as Orleans Parish, LA; Harris County, TX; and Santa Clara County, CA.

The importance of this moment notwithstanding, there is still more bad news than good when it comes to pretrial justice. Even amid all of the attention and policy change, half a million legally innocent people are sitting in jail *on any given day* in this country. While there is limited data on the total number of people detained pretrial over the course of a year, given the relatively short duration of most pretrial detentions, the number undoubtedly reaches into the millions.

Moreover, while the policy reforms referenced above are a critical shift after decades of policy and practice that showed a total disregard for the extraordinary human toll of pretrial detention, most of the changes are relatively limited in scope and continue to place far more emphasis on the somewhat abstract notion of "risk" than on actual legal innocence and documented harm of pretrial detention. More-over, even these limited reforms have been subject to intense, immediate backlash and some have already been undone.

In California, Senate Bill (SB) 10: The Money Bail Reform Act, which was passed by the state legislature and signed by the governor in 2018, made California the first state to fully eliminate cash bail. In this case however, the backlash began long before the reform passed, as vocal opposition by prosecutors, judges, and other criminal justice professionals as well as many legislators resulted in dramatic revisions to the bill while it was debated and negotiated in the legislature. The version that ultimately passed drew the ire of both pro-bail constituencies, such as the bail bond industry, and much of the criminal justice reform movement, which objected to replacing cash bail with a "risk-based system" as determined by an algorithmic "risk assessment instrument" (SB 10). In November 2020, an unlikely coalition that included the bail bond industry and many Black Lives Matter organizations overturned California's bail reform law in a statewide ballot referendum.

Similarly, the bail reform that the Alaska state legislature passed in 2016 has also been reversed. SB 91, a broad criminal justice reform bill intended to reduce the state's rapidly growing prison and jail populations through changes to sentencing, probation, parole, and pretrial detention practices, was subjected to an immediate backlash, as law enforcement and lawmakers blamed the changes for spikes in property crime, despite research indicating a spurious connection. The new law became a central issue in the 2018 gubernatorial election and when Gov. Mike Dunleavy was elected with a promise to "Make Alaska Safe Again," he used an executive order to undo most of SB 91's reforms, including bail reform.

A multiyear, multi-bill bail reform battle in Illinois underscores the contentiousness of bail reform politics and the uncertainty as to whether pro- or anti-reform advocates will prevail. In 2017, Illinois passed the Bail Reform Act, which recommended limitations on the use of money bail and consideration for people's ability to pay, but still allowed almost total discretion for judges and prosecutors without any mandates related to bail affordability or pretrial release. Despite the limited scope of this law, in 2019, several Illinois state representatives introduced House Bill (HB) 221, which would have allowed counties with fewer than 3,000,000 residents—in other words, all but Cook County—to opt-out of the 2017 bail reform law. Although the bill did not make it out the legislative committee process, the fact that it was carried by eight co-sponsors makes clear the level of support it had. Nonetheless, in 2021, pro-reform legislators passed another bail-related bill, the Pretrial Fairness Act, a sweeping piece of legislation that seeks to fully eliminate cash bail and puts the state at the forefront of pretrial justice. While rollbacks in California and Alaska demonstrate the fragility of these reforms, it is nonetheless a huge milestone for the reform movement.

Notwithstanding efforts to undo bail reform in some states, there are bail and pretrial justice reforms that are still promising, including New York State's Bail Elimination Act, which, in spite of some rollbacks, still goes significantly further than most bail re-form legislation by mandating nonmonetary release for a wide array of offenses, including most misdemeanors and nonviolent felonies as well as a couple of violent felonies. New Jersey's Criminal Jus-tice Reform Act of 2017 is also a critical success story. New Jersey, like California, replaced the state's cash-based system with a "risk-based" system, but, unlike California, has a strong presumption of release and much more limited circumstances that require or allow for detention.[3]

A growing movement to reform the practice of criminal prose-cution has also identified bail reform and pretrial justice as central issues for prosecutors to address.[4] Notwithstanding the growing use of the term "progressive prosecution" to describe this mindset, local prosecutors from both Republican and Democratic jurisdictions are increasingly changing their own policies and practices and support-ing legislative reform.

Taken together, the array of advocacy and policy change make clear that we are simultaneously at a moment of great opportunity and one of great risk. If we can harness the renewed awareness to our current state of injustice to achieve meaningful, substantial pretrial policy change, we can reduce the unjust detention of the uncon-victed and, in so doing, attack mass incarceration. On the other hand, if we miss or misuse this opportunity, we risk not only perpet-uating existing injustice, but also further undermining the meaning of innocence by implementing ostensibly objective actuarial tools that exchange the presumption of innocence for some notion of "risk" that is both inherently abstract and fundamentally dismissive of the risk pretrial detention brings to the accused. In this context, I hope *Incarceration without Conviction* can serve to bear witness to the wrongs of pretrial detention and thus contribute to the movement for pretrial justice.

Notes

1 https://joebiden.com/justice/#
2 As discussed below, Alaska's bail reforms have since been largely reversed and California's were defeated in a statewide referendum.
3 The new law also includes provisions requiring faster case processing, since lengthy case processing times result in longer detentions for individuals held in custody. For a full description of the changes made and their effect on pretrial case processing, see Anderson et al. (2019) and the New Jersey Courts' Criminal Justice Reform Information Center: https://njcourts.gov/courts/criminal/reform.html
4 See, for example, Fair and Just Prosecution's Issues at a Glance Brief on bail reform: https://fairandjustprosecution.org/wp-content/uploads/2017/09/FJPBrief.BailReform.9.25.pdf

Appendix
Notes on Quantitative Methodology

I used logistic regression models to calculate the relationship between various defendant and case characteristics on two key outcomes: the odds of being detained pretrial and the odds of being convicted. The latter, as shown in Tables 2.1 and 2.5, measures the effects of a variety of independent variables associated with criminal conviction on the dependent variable conviction.

Conviction is a binary outcome, coded as 0/1 with 0 indicating that a defendant was not convicted of any charges and 1 indicating that a defendant was convicted of at least one felony. The primary independent variable of interest is pretrial detention status, coded as 0/1 for not detained / detained. This model also includes variables for race, which is coded as 0/1 for not Black and Black;[1] age (represented as a log of the defendant's age); and legal variables for type of counsel (public defender = 1, private attorney = 0) and number of charges by offense type (number of drug charges, weapons charges, violent charges and property charges).[2]

In the other analysis, as shown in Table 2.4, pretrial detention status is examined as a dependent variable, with all other covariates as independent variables. Pretrial detention is constructed as a binary outcome, coded as 0/1 for not detained throughout adjudication / detained throughout adjudication. Table 1.1 in Chapter 1 provides descriptions for defendant characteristic variables. The remaining variables are described in Table A.1 below.

Table A.1 Offense variable descriptions

Name	Coding	Mean	Range	SD
Drugs	Number of drug charges	0.97	0–19	1.25
Weapons	Number of weapons charges	0.43	0–17	1.47
Property	Number of property charges	0.23	0–15	0.88
Violent	Number of violent charges	0.41	0–26	1.97

Notes

1 There are not sufficient numbers of any racial/ethnic groups other than Blacks processed through the Cook County Circuit Courts or in this dataset to allow for dummy variables for racial groups other than Black and not Black. Because extensive research has demonstrated that Black Americans have worse criminal justice outcomes than all other racial groups, I have followed dominant practices in criminal justice research by categorizing all defendants as Black or not Black, rather than White and not White, as is more common in other areas of quantitative research.

2 Most models on criminal justice outcomes create dummy variables for each defendant's most serious charge instead of continuous variables for the number of charges of each type, but this strategy has two shortcomings. First, there is no "standard" offense, so choosing which offense to use as a reference category is generally an arbitrary decision, which nonetheless influences the interpretation of a model. Second, prosecutors often charge defendants with the maximum possible number of offenses in order to create leverage for plea bargains, indicating that the number of offenses a defendant is charged with, as well as the type and severity of these charges, probably affects his/her case outcome (Gaines and Miller 2019).

References

Adams, Kenneth. 1992. "Adjusting to Prison Life." In M. Tonry (Ed.), *Crime and Justice: A Review of Research*, pp. 276–359. Chicago, IL: University of Chicago Press.

Alexander, Michelle. 2012. *The New Jim Crow: Mass Incarceration in the Age of Colorblindness*. New York, NY: The New Press.

Anderson, Chloe, Cindy Redcross, Erin Valentine, and Luke Miratrix. 2019. *Pretrial Justice Reform Study: Evaluation of Pretrial Justice System Reform That Use the Public Safety Assessment: Effects of New Jersey's Criminal Justice Reform*. New York, NY: MDRC Center for Criminal Justice.

Bazelon, Emily. 2019. *Charged: The New Movement to Transform American Prosecution and End Mass Incarceration*. New York, NY: Random House.

Beckett, Katherine. 1997. *Making Crime Pay: Law and Order in Contemporary American Politics*. New York, NY: Oxford University Press.

Beckett, Katherine A., Alexes M. Harris, and Heather Evans. 2008. *The Assessment and Consequences of Legal Financial Obligations in Washington State: Research Report*. Olympia, WA: Washington State Minority and Justice Commission.

Bell v. Wolfish. 1979. 441 US 520.

Bock, E. Wilbur and Charles E. Frazier. 1977. "Official Standards versus Actual Criteria in Bond Disposition." *Journal of Criminal Justice*. 5(4): 321–328.

Boshier, R and Derek Johnson, 1974. "Does Conviction Affect Employment Opportunities?" *British Journal of Criminology*. 14: 264–268.

Bradford, Ben. 2014. "Policing and Social Identity: Procedural Justice, Inclusion and Cooperation between Police and Public." *Policing and Society*. 24(1): 22–43.

Brockett, Jr, William A. 1971. "Presumed Guilty: The Pre-Trial Detainee." *Yale Review of Law and Social Action*. 1(4): 1–18.

Buikhuisen, W. and E. P. H. Dijksterhuis. 1971. "Delinquency and Stagmatisation." *British Journal of Criminology*. 11: 185–187.

Coffin v. United States. 1895. 156 US 432.

Cole, George F. and Charles H. Logan. 1977. "Parole: The Consumer's Perspective." *Criminal Justice Review*. 2(2): 71–80.

Devers, Lindsey. 2011. "Plea and Charge Bargaining: Research Summary," *Bureau of Justice Assistance Report*. Washington, DC: Department of Justice.

Eason, Michael J. 1988. "Eighth Amendment—Pretrial Detention: What Will Become of the Innocent." *Journal of Criminal Law & Criminology*. 78(4): 1048–1079.

Eisenstein, James and Herbert Jacob. 1977. *Felony Justice: An Organizational Analysis of Criminal Courts*. Boston, MA: Little, Brown and Company, Inc.

Ervin, Jr, Sam J. 1971. "Foreword: Preventive Detention—A Step Backward for Criminal Justice." *Harvard Civil Liberties-Civil Rights Law Review*. 6(2): 291–299.

Foote, Caleb. 1954. "Compelling Appearance in Court: Administration of Bail in Philadelphia." *University of Pennsylvania Law Review*. 102: 1031–1079.

Foote, Caleb. 1958a. "Forward: Comment on the New York Bail Study." *University of Pennsylvania Law Review*. 106: 685–692.

Foote, Caleb. 1958b. "A Study of the Administration of Bail in New York City." *University of Pennsylvania Law Review*. 106: 693–730.

Foote, Caleb. 1959. "The Bail System and Equal Justice." *Federal Probation*. 23: 43–48.

Foote, Caleb. 1965a. "The Coming Constitutional Crisis in Bail: I." *University of Pennsylvania Law Review*. 113: 959–999.

Foote, Caleb. 1965b. "The Coming Constitutional Crisis in Bail: II." *University of Pennsylvania Law Review*. 113: 1125–1185.

Freed, Daniel J. and Patricia M. Wald. 1964. *Bail in the United States, 1964*. Washington, DC: National Conference on Bail and Criminal Justice.

Gaines, Larry K. and Roger LeRoy Miller. 2019. *Criminal Justice in Action*. 10th edn. Boston, MA: Cengage.

Goldkamp, John S. 1979. *Two Classes of Accused: A Study of Bail and Detention in American Justice*. Cambridge, MA: Ballinger Publishing Company.

Goldkamp, John S. 1985. "Danger and Detention: A Second Generation of Bail Reform." *Journal of Criminal Law and Criminology*. 76(1): 1–74.

Goldkamp, John S. and Michael R. Gottfredson. 1979. "Bail Decision Making and Pretrial Detention." *Law and Human Behavior*. 3: 227–249.

Goldkamp, John S., Michael R. Gottfredson, Peter R. Jones, and Doris Weiland. 1995. *Personal Liberty and Community Safety. The Plenum Series in Crime and Justice*. Boston, MA: Springer.

Goodstein, Lynne. 1980. "Psychological Effects of the Predictability of Prison Release Implications for the Sentencing Debate." *Criminology*. 18(3): 363–384.

Gramlich, John. 2017. "Federal Criminal Prosecutions Fall to Lowest Level In Nearly Two Decades." In *Fact Tank: News in the Numbers*. Washington, DC: Pew Research Center.

Gramlich, John. 2019. "Only 2% of Federal Criminal Defendants Go to Trial, and Most Who Do Are Found Guilty." In *Fact Tank: News in the Numbers*. Washington, DC: Pew Research Center.

Grogger, Jeffrey. 1992. "The Effect of Arrests on the Employment and Earnings of Young Men." *The Quarterly Journal of Economics*. 110(1): 51–71.

Hagan, John and Ronit Dinovitzer. 1999. "Collateral Consequences of Imprisonment for Children, Communities, and Prisoners." *Crime and Justice*. 26: 121–162.

Haney, Craig. 2002. "The Psychological Impact of Incarceration: Implications for Post-Prison Adjustment." Paper presented at *From Prison to Home: The Effect of Incarceration and Reentry on Children, Families and Communities*. Washington, DC: US Department of Health and Human Services, The Urban Institute.

Haney, Craig. 2006. *Reforming Punishment: Psychological Limits to the Pains of Imprisonment*. Washington, DC: American Psychological Association.

Hart, Michelle E. 2006. "Race, Sentencing, and the Pretrial Process." Unpublished Dissertation. Retrieved from https://drum.lib.umd.edu/handle/1903/4063

Heaton, Paul, Sandra Mayson, and Megan Stevenson. 2017. "The Downstream Consequences of Misdemeanor Pretrial Detention." *Stanford Law Review*. 61(3): 711.

Hirschel, David, Eve Buzawa, April Pattavina, and Don Faggiani. 2007. "Domestic Violence and Mandatory Arrest Laws: To What Extent Do They Influence Police Arrest Decisions?" *Journal of Criminal Law and Criminology*. 98(1): 255–298.

Jones, Arnold P. 1989. "Criminal Bail: How Bail Reform is Working in Selected District Courts." Testimony Before the Subcommittee on the Constitution Committee on the Judiciary United States Senate.

Jones, Rick, Geralld B. Lefcourt, Barry J. Pollack, Normal L. Reimer, and Kyle O'Dowd. 2018. *The Trial Penalty: The Sixth Amendment Right to Trial on the Verge of Extinction and How to Save It*. Washington, DC: National Association of Criminal Defense Lawyers.

Kajstura, Aleks. 2019. *Women's Mass Incarceration: The Whole Pie 2019*. Washington, DC: Prison Policy Institute.

Kohler-Hausmann, Issa. 2018. *Misdemeanorland: Criminal Courts and Social Control in an Age of Broken Windows Policing*. Princeton, NJ: Princeton University Press.

Lowenkamp, Christopher T., Marie VanNostrand, and Alexander Holsinger. 2013. *The Hidden Costs of Pretrial Detention*. Houston, TX: Laura and John Arthur Foundation.

MacDonald, John and Steven Raphael. 2017. *An Analysis of Racial and Ethnic Disparities in Case Dispositions and Sentencing Outcomes for Criminal Cases Presented to and Processed by the Office of the San Francisco District Attorney*. www.courthousenews.com/wp-content/uploads/2018/01/RacialDisparities.pdf

MacKenzie, Doris L. and Lynne Goodstein. 1985. "Long-Term Incarceration Impacts and Characteristics of Long-Term Offenders: An Empirical Analysis." *Criminal Justice and Behavior*. 12(4): 395–414.

Martin, Karin D., Bryan L. Sykes, Sarah Shannon, Frank Edwards, and Alexes Harris. 2018. "Monetary Sanctions: Legal Financial Obligations in US Systems of Justice." *Annual Review of Criminology*. 1: 471–495.

Martinez, Brandon P., Nick Petersen, and Marisa Omori. 2020. "Time, Money, and Punishment: Institutional Racial-Ethnic Inequalities in Pretrial Detention and Case Outcomes." *Crime and Delinquency*. 66(6–7): 1–27.

Mason, Gary L. 1990. "Indeterminate Sentencing: Cruel and Unusual Punishment, or Just Plain Cruel?" *New England Journal of Criminal and Civil Confinement*. 16: 89–120.

Mauer, Marc. 1999. *Race to Incarcerate*. New York, NY: New Press.

Mauer, Marc and Meda Chesney-Lind. 2002. *Invisible Punishment: The Collateral Consequences of Mass Imprisonment*. New York, NY: New Press.

Meares, Tracey. 2009. "The Legitimacy of Police among Young African-American Men." *Marquette Law Review*. 92(4): 651–666.

Messinger, Sheldon L., and Phillip E. Johnson. 1978. "Determinate Sentencing: Reform or Regression?" Presentation at *California's Determinate Sentencing Statute: History and Issues*. Berkeley, CA: National Institute of Law Enforcement and Criminal Justice, US Department of Justice.

Middlemass, Keesha. 2017. *Convicted and Condemned: The Politics and Policies of Prisoner Reentry*. New York, NY: New York University Press.

Miller, Marc and Martin Guggenheim. 1990. "Pretrial Detention and Punishment." *Minnesota Law Review*. 75: 335–426.

Miller, Paul E. 1970. "Preventive Detention: A Guide to the Eradication of Individual Rights." *Howard Law Journal*. 16(1). Retrieved from https://heinonline.org/HOL/LandingPage?handle=hein.journals/howlj16&div=11&id=&page=

Minton, Todd D. and William J. Sabol. 2009. "Jail Inmates at Midyear 2008 – Statistical Tables." *Bureau of Justice Statistics*. Washington, DC: US Department of Justice.

Natapoff, Alexandra. 2018. *Punishment without Crime: How Our Massive Misdemeanor System Traps the Innocent and Makes America More Unequal*. New York, NY: Basic Books.

Nellis, Ashley. 2016. *The Color of Justice: Racial and Ethnic Disparity in State Prisons*. Washington, DC: The Sentencing Project.

Oleski, Martin S. 1977. "The Effect of Indefinite Pretrial Incarceration on the Anxiety Level of an Urban Jail Population." *Journal of Clinical Psychology*. 33: 1006–1008.

Oleson, James C., Christopher T. Lowenkamp, Timothy P. Cadigan, Marie VanNostrand and John Wooldredge. 2014. "The Effect of Pretrial Detention on Sentencing in Two Federal Districts" *Justice Quarterly*, 33(6): 1103–1122.

Omori, Marisa and Nick Petersen. 2020. "Institutionalizing Inequality in the Courts: Decomposing Racial and Ethnic Disparities in Detention, Conviction, and Sentencing." *Criminology*. 58(4): 678–713.

Pager, Devah. 2003. "The Mark of a Criminal Record." *American Journal of Sociology.* 108(5): 937–975.

Pager, Devah. 2007. *Marked: Race, Crime, and Finding Work in an Era of Mass Incarceration.* Chicago, IL: University of Chicago Press.

Pager, Devah and Lincoln Quillian. 2005. "Walking the Talk? What Employers Say Versus What They Do." *American Sociological Review.* 70(3): 355–380.

Patillo, Mary, David Weiman, and Bruce Western (eds). 2004. *Imprisoning America: The Social Effects of Mass Incarceration.* New York, NY: Russell Sage Foundation.

Perkins, Craig A., James J. Stephan, and Allen Beck. 1995. "Census of Jails and Annual Survey of Jails: Jails and Jail Inmates 1993–94." In *Bureau of Justice Statistics Bulletin.* Washington, DC: US Department of Justice.

Petersen, Nick. 2019a. "Do Detainees Plead Guilty Faster? A Survival Analysis of Pretrial Detention and the Timing of Guilty Pleas." *Criminal Justice Policy Review.* 31(7): 1015–1035.

Petersen, Nick. 2019b. "Low-Level, but High Speed? Assessing Pretrial Detention Effects on the Timing and Content of Misdemeanor versus Felony Guilty Pleas." *Justice Quarterly.* 36(7): 1314–1335.

Petersen, Nick. 2020. "Cumulative Racial and Ethnic Inequalities in Potentially Capital Cases: A Multi-Stage Analysis of Pre-trial Disparities." *Criminal Justice Review.* 45(2): 225–249.

Petersen, Nick and Marisa Omori. 2020. "Is the Process the Only Punishment? Racial-Ethnic Disparities in Lower-Level Courts." *Law & Policy.* 42(1): 1–22.

Pfaff, John. 2014. "Escaping from the Standard Story: Why the Conventional Wisdom on Prison Growth is Wrong, and Where We Can Go From Here." *Federal Sentencing Reporter.* 26(4): 265–270.

Pfaff, John. 2017. *Locked In: The True Causes of Mass Incarceration—and How to Achieve Real Reform.* New York, NY: Basic Books.

Pfaff, John. 2020. "Theories of Mass Imprisonment." *Criminal Justice Theory, Vol. 26: Explanations and Effects.* New York, NY: Routledge.

Phillips, Mary. 2007. *Pretrial Detention and Case Outcomes, Part 1: Nonfelony Cases.* New York: New York City Criminal Justice Agency. www.nycja. org/assets/NonFelonyDetentionOutcomes07.pdf

Phillips, Mary. 2008. *Pretrial Detention and Case Outcomes, Part 2: Felony Cases.* New York: New York City Criminal Justice Agency. www.nycja. org/publications/pretrial-detention-and-case-outcomes-part-2-felony-cases

Phillips, Mary. 2012. *A Decade of Bail Research in New York City.* New York: New York City Criminal Justice Agency. www.prisonpolicy.org/scans/DecadeBailResearch12.pdf

Porporino, Frank J. 1992. "Behavior and Adaptation in Long-Term Prison Inmates: Descriptive Longitudinal Results." *Criminal Justice and Behavior.* 19(4): 409–425.

Porporino, Frank J. and Edward Zamble. 1984. "Coping with Imprisonment." *Canadian Journal of Criminology*. 26(4): 403–421.

President's Task Force on 21st Century Policing. 2015. *Final Report of the President's Task Force on 21st Century Policing*. Washington, DC: Office of Community Oriented Policing Services.

Quattlebaum, Megan, Tracey Meares, and Tom Tyler. 2018. *Principles of Procedurally Just Policing*. Princeton, NJ: The Justice Collaboratory.

Rankin, Anne. 1964. "The Effect of Pretrial Detention." *New York University Law Review*. 39: 641–655.

Rosenfeld, Richard, and Robert Fornango. 2014. "The Impact of Police Stops on Precinct Robbery and Burglary Rates in New York City, 2003–2010." *Justice Quarterly*. 31: 132–158.

Sacks, Meghan and Alissa R. Ackerman. 2012. "Pretrial Detention and Guilty Pleas: If They Cannot Afford Bail They Must Be Guilty." *Criminal Justice Studies: A Critical Journal of Crime, Law, and Society*. 25(3): 265–278.

Schlesinger, Traci. 2007. "The Cumulative Effects of Racial Disparities in Criminal Processing." *The Journal of the Institute of Justice & International Studies*. 7: 261–278.

Schoenfeld, Heather. 2018. *Building the Prison State: Race and the Politics of Mass Incarceration*. Chicago, IL: University of Chicago Press.

Schwartz, Richard D. and Jerome H. Skolnick. "Two Studies of Legal Stigma." *Social Problems*. 10(2): 133–142.

Shannon, Sarah, Beth M. Huebner, Alexes Harris, Karin Martin, Mary Pattillo, Becky Pettit, Bryan Sykes, and Christopher Uggen. 2020. "The Broad Scope and Variation of Monetary Sanctions: Evidence from Eight States." *UCLA Criminal Justice Law Review*. 4(1): 269–281.

Solomon, Amy. 2012. "Briefing on the Impact of Criminal Background Checks and the EEOC's Conviction Records Policy on the Employment of Black and Hispanic Workers." Washington, DC: US Department of Justice.

Stack v. Boyle. 1951. 342 US 1, 72 S. Ct. 1.

Stanford SPARQ. 2018. *Principled Policing: Procedural Justice and Implicit Bias Training*. Retrieved from https://stanford.app.box.com/s/e3ik3z20be2k9k6p6pluo9o42wdz5cni

Subramanian, Ram, Ruth Delaney, Stephen Roberts, Nancy Fishman, and Peggy McGarry. 2015a. *Incarceration's Front Door: The Misuse of Jails in America*. New York, NY: Vera Institute of Justice.

Subramanian, Ram, Christian Henrichson, and Jacob Kang-Brown. 2015b. *In Our Own Backyard: Confronting Growth and Disparities in American Jails*. New York, NY: Vera Institute of Justice.

Sunshine, Jason and Tom R. Tyler. 2003. "The Role of Procedural Justice and Legitimacy in Shaping Public Support for Policing." *Law and Society Review*, 37: 555–589.

Sykes, Gresham. 1958/2007. *The Society of Captives: A Study of a Maximum Security Prison*. Princeton, NJ: Princeton University Press.

Thaler, Jeff. 1978. "Punishing the Innocent: The Need for Due Process and the Presumption of Innocence Prior to Trial." *Wisconsin Law Review.* 441(2): 441–484.

Thomas, Wayne H. 1976. *Bail Reform in America.* Berkeley, CA: University of California Press.

Toborg, Mary. 1981. *Pretrial Release: A National Evaluation of Practices and Outcomes.* Washington, DC: US Department of Justice, National Institute of Justice.

Travis, Jeremy, Bruce Western, and Steve Redburn (Eds.). 2014. *The Growth of Incarceration in the United States: Exploring Causes and Consequences.* Committee on Causes and Consequences of High Rates of Incarceration, Committee on Law and Justice, Division of Behavioral and Social Sciences and Education. Washington, DC: The National Academies Press.

Tyler, Tom R. 2003. "Procedural Justice, Legitimacy, and the Effective Rule of Law." *Crime and Justice.* 30: 283–357.

Tyler, Tom R. 2017. "Procedural Justice and Policing: A Rush to Judgment?" *Annual Review of Law and Social Science.* 13: 29–53.

Uggen, Christopher, Mike Vuolo, Sarah Lageson, Ebony Ruhland, and Hilary K. Whitham. 2014. "The Edge of Stigma: An Experimental Audit of the Effects of Low Level Criminal Records on Unemployment." *Criminology.* 52(4): 627–654.

US v. Salerno. 1987. 481 US 739.

Van Cleeve, Nicole G. 2016. *Crook County: Racism and Injustice in America's Largest Criminal Court.* Stanford, CA: Stanford University Press.

Wald, Patricia M. and David J. Freed. 1966. 'The Bail Reform Act of 1966: A Practitioner's Primer." *American Bar Association Journal.* 52(10): 940–945.

Waldfogel, Joel. 1994. "Does Conviction Have a Persistent Effect on Income and Employment?" *International Review of Law and Economics.* 14(1): 103–119.

Walker, Julian, C. Illingworth, A. Canning, E. Garner, J. Wooley, P. Taylor, and T. Amos. 2014. "Changes in Mental State Associated with Prison Environments: A Systematic Review." *Acta Psychiatrica.* 129: 427–436.

Wanger, Betsy K. 1987. "Limiting Preventive Detention through Conditional Release: The Unfulfilled Promise of the 1982 Pretrial Services Act." *The Yale Law Journal.* 97: 320–340.

Western, Bruce. 2002. "The Impact of Incarceration on Wage Mobility and Inequality." *American Sociological Review.* 67(4): 526–546.

Western, Bruce and Becky Petit. 2005. "Black-White Wage Inequality, Employment Rates, and Incarceration." *American Journal of Sociology.* 111: 553–578.

Western, Bruce, Jeffrey R. Kling, and David F. Weiman. 2001. "The Labor Market Consequences of Incarceration." *Crime & Delinquency.* 47(3): 410–427.

Western, Bruce, Leonard M. Lopoo, and Sarah McLanahan. 2004. "Incarceration and the Bonds between Parents in Fragile Families." In Mary

E. Pattillo, David E. Weinmen, and Bruce Western (Eds.), *Imprisoning America: The Social Consequences of Mass Incarceration*, pp. 21–45. New York, NY: Russell Sage.

Williams, Marian R. 2003. "The Effect of Pretrial Detention on Imprisonment Decisions." *Criminal Justice Review.* 28(2): 299–316.

Zamble, Ed. 1988. *Coping, Behavior, and Adaptation in Prison Inmates.* New York and Berlin: Springer-Verlag.

Zamble, Ed. 1992. "Behavior and Adaptation in Long-Term Prison Inmates: Descriptive Longitudinal Results." *Criminal Justice and Behavior*, 19: 409–425.

Zamble, Ed and Frank Porporino. 1990. "Coping, Imprisonment, and Rehabilitation: Some Data and their Implications." *Criminal Justice and Behavior.* 17: 53–70.

Zamble, Ed, Frank Porporino, and Julia Kalotay. 1984. "An Analysis of Coping Behavior in Prison Inmates." *Programs Branch User Report, No. 1984–77.* Ottawa: Ministry of the Solicitor General.

Index

Note: **Bold** page numbers refer to tables and page numbers followed by "n" denote endnotes.